Abounding in Hope

A *Family of Faith* at *Work through* the *Lutheran World Federation*

CHARLES P. LUTZ

AUGSBURG Publishing House • Minneapolis

ABOUNDING IN HOPE
A Family of Faith at Work through the Lutheran World Federation

Scripture quotations unless otherwise noted are from the Revised Standard Version of the Bible, copyright 1946, 1952, and 1971 by the Division of Christian Education of the National Council of Churches.

Scripture quotations marked TEV are from The Good News Bible, Today's English Version, copyright 1966, 1971, 1976 by American Bible Society. Used by permission.

English quotations from the Lutheran Confessions are from the *Book of Concord*, translated and edited by Theodore G. Tappert, © 1959 by Fortress Press (formerly Muhlenberg Press).

Photos: Peter Williams, pp. 4, 24, 28, 38, 56, 62, 82, 90, 98, 110, 114, 118, 126, 142 (top); Lutheran Standard, p. 8; Tibor Moldoványi, pp. 44, 74; Herb David, p. 142 (bottom).

Library of Congress Cataloging in Publication Data

Lutz, Charles P.
  ABOUNDING IN HOPE.

  Bibliography: p.
  1. Lutheran World Federation.   I. Title.
BX8004.L93L87 1985   284.1   85-1216
ISBN 0-8066-2158-3

Manufactured in the U.S.A.   APH 10-0123

1 2 3 4 5 6 7 8 9 0 1 2 3 4 5 6 7 8 9

Contents

Bishop Zoltan Kaldy of the Hungarian Lutheran Church, president of the Lutheran World Federation, with his wife Magdolna, a university professor in Budapest.

Introduction

This book has a single goal. It seeks to involve you, the reader, in a magnificent story. Know it or not, you are a part of that story if you are a member of a Lutheran congregation. You are a member of the family of faith whose story is being told here.

The book is about the worldwide Lutheran family and what it is thinking and doing today. It is written to bring close what seems distant, to give local meaning to that which is global, to make personal those wings and activities of the family which we have not fully known.

We tell the story through the prism of an event: two weeks during the summer of 1984 in Budapest, capital city of Hungary. But our story is not primarily that of a meeting. Rather, the meeting is the occasion for looking at what the Lutheran family is up to these days.

The meeting in Budapest was an assembly, the seventh held since 1947, of the Lutheran World Federation. The Lutheran World Federation (LWF) is an association of churches around the world, 99 of them in 49 countries. This book will tell you something about the work you and your congregation are doing through that organization.

The book can be used for individual reading or it can be the basis for study and discussion by a group.

If you use it for group discussion, here are some suggestions:

1. Get copies enough for each member of the group.
2. Order other written or audiovisual materials you may want to use (check items listed in chapter notes and Appendix 3).
3. Ask participants to read a chapter prior to each session (there are eight chapters, so you will likely want at least eight sessions).
4. As a pattern for each session's discussion you could follow this sequence:
● invite general sharing: What in the text was striking to people, or surprising, or disturbing, or satisfying, or made them glad, sad, angry, perplexed, or curious?
● discuss the quotations that open each chapter;
● talk about the "Words to Ponder" that close each chapter;
● discuss the questions listed under "For Discussion."

The group study could have one person serving as leader throughout, or the leadership could be shared among several persons.

Whether you read the book alone or study it as part of a group, I hope you enjoy the experience and become better acquainted with this family called "Lutheran."

I pray also that your reading will help you to "be prepared to make a defense to any one who calls you to account for the hope that is in you" (1 Peter 3:15).

One cautionary word: in addition to factual information on LWF work and the actions of the Budapest Assembly, this book contains opinions by the author; for those the LWF is not responsible.

And a word of gratitude to those who reviewed the manuscript and made helpful suggestions: John Bachman, Jim Bergquist, David Burke, Marc Chambron, Herb David,

Elaine Donaldson, Dennis Frado, Fern Lee Hagedorn, Paul A. Hanson, Bonnie Jensen, George S. Johnson, Frances Maher, Mark Thomsen, and Paul Wee.

I also wish to thank David W. Preus, presiding bishop of The American Lutheran Church, who encouraged and supported me in undertaking this writing task. He also provided key leadership at the Assembly, as an effective presiding officer in many plenary sessions and as a leader in the LWF's Executive Committee.

Finally, I thank the ALC and its Standing Committee for Church in Society, which agreed to contribute six weeks of my time to attendance at the Budapest Assembly and the writing of this book. I dedicate it to the members of the Standing Committee and to my colleagues in the Office of Church in Society, who willingly and professionally assumed many added tasks during my absence.

CHARLES P. LUTZ
Minneapolis, Minnesota
USA

Hungarian women in traditional dress arrive for the opening service of the LWF Seventh Assembly in Budapest. The banner on the sports hall reads: "7th Evangelical World Assembly."

1

Who Are the Members of This Family?

"A Christian is a perfectly free lord of all, subject to none. A Christian is a perfectly dutiful servant of all, subject to all."
—*Martin Luther,* The Freedom of a Christian, *Luther's Works, vol. 31 (Fortress, 1957), p. 344*

"For it is by God's grace that you have been saved through faith. It is not the result of your own efforts, but God's gift, so that no one can boast about it. God has made us what we are, and in our union with Christ Jesus he has created us for a life of good deeds, which he has already prepared for us to do."
—*Ephesians 2:8-10 TEV*

These people called "Lutheran." Who are they? Where do they live? With all their differences, what unites them? And why do they use *that* name, anyway, if they claim to be worshipers of Jesus Christ?

This chapter—a look at the global family known as Lutherans—will address such questions as these.

In many ways Lutherans are like a family, a vast, extended family. We live in about 100 different nations of the world; there are, at last count, organized Lutheran churches in 87 countries, and scattered Lutheran people are present in many others.

The family numbers just under 70,000,000 members, making us the largest Protestant family among the world's Christians. (Roman Catholics are the most numerous, with more than 600,000,000, and Eastern Orthodox Christians total approximately 68,000,000.)

We are a diverse family. We have our disagreements, even an occasional divorce. Some wings of the family think that other wings aren't faithful enough to the family identity. Still other parts of the family are embarrassed because they think the words or deeds of certain kinfolk give the whole family a bad name.

Certainly there is much on which the Lutheran family does not agree. We don't speak the same language. We live in many and varied cultures and under a diversity of social systems. We don't all worship in the same style. We don't have the same views on church government, ordination of women, or how the church should relate to society. We don't all even use the same family name.

What unites the family?

Yet in spite of all these differences there is a thread of unity that keeps people together in this family. It's an approach to the Christian faith. We are known as a *confessional* church, meaning that we are tied together because of a particular confession of that faith.

The basic expression of the faith to which all Lutherans subscribe is the Augsburg Confession. Some parts of the family, in fact, name themselves officially after that statement of faith, rather than after the 16th-century reformer Martin Luther. The Augsburg Confession is a document that was presented to Emperor Charles V in the Bavarian city of Augsburg on June 25, 1530, by German princes who followed Martin Luther's teachings. It expresses the understanding of Christian faith which differentiated the followers of Luther from others in the Western or Roman Catholic tradition.

Members of the Lutheran family also accept as correct expressions of the biblical faith two "catechisms" or guides to instruction by Luther: the Small Catechism and the Large Catechism, both published in 1529. In addition, Lutherans claim as part of their confessional library three other documents from the 16th century: the Apology (defense) of the Augsburg Confession, The Smalcald Articles, and the Formula of Concord. (We also confess, along with most other Christians, the three ecumenical creeds from earlier centuries: Apostles', Nicene, and Athanasian.) As the basis for these confessions of faith and all of its theological work, Lutheranism looks to the Holy Scriptures. The writings of the Old and New Testaments are the highest authority for guiding our faith and life.

The reform movement started by Martin Luther originally did not see itself as creating a separate church. It sought rather to change the existing Western church by recovering certain basic biblical emphases. The Conclusion to the Augsburg Confession tried to make that clear:

> Only those things have been recounted which it seemed necessary to say in order that it may be understood that nothing has been received among us, in doctrine or in ceremonies, that is contrary to Scripture or to the church catholic. For it is manifest that we have guarded diligently against the introduction into our churches of any new and ungodly doctrines.

The confessors at Augsburg wanted their churches' teachings to be viewed as a corrective movement within the one, holy, catholic, and apostolic church, returning it to the path of biblical faith from which it had strayed.

Even to this day, after separate "Lutheran" churches have existed for 450 years, there is a strong yearning among many Lutherans for reunion with other Christians. Lutherans are among the leaders in pursuing faith dialog with other Christian groups, always seeking a basis for reconciliation (see Chapter 4). The Augsburg Confession states that, for the true unity of the church, "it is enough to agree concerning the teaching of the Gospel and the administration of the Sacraments."[1] Lutherans, therefore, have never claimed that a separate church called "Lutheran" should be a permanent goal.

And yet there continue to be distinctive emphases which characterize the Lutheran way of confessing Christ. (Some of these are summarized at the beginning of Chapter 2.) And it is not surprising that these emphases emerge from the experience of the monk Martin Luther and his search for a gracious God. As a young man, Luther was tormented by his sense of unworthiness and his inability to find acceptance in God's eyes.

The breakthrough for Luther, which he later likened to having been "born again," came through his study of St. Paul's letters, especially Romans and Galatians. There he found that God declares human beings to be acceptable ("justified") on the basis of faith in Christ's redeeming work. This justification came through faith *alone*, apart from deeds that we do or do not perform. That biblical rediscovery by Luther has, to this day, marked people called Lutherans. It is our great strength and undoubtedly our chief contribution to the grand mosaic of Christian theologies: to call the faithful always back to the centrality of God's redeeming activity, to *grace* and not our merit before God, to *faith* in Christ rather than works that we do to gain salvation.

And yet, tragically, the centrality of grace has at times been misunderstood among Lutherans, leading us into ethical indifference or social and political quietism. Sometimes Lutherans have concluded that, if there is nothing we can do to win God's favor, there is nothing we should do at all! If good works are worthless for earning divine approval, good works on behalf of my neighbor in need also may be ignored—or at least be seen as optional. To this day, Lutherans struggle with—and disagree about—the ethical and social consequences of "justification by grace through faith alone."

What names do we bear?

If, as a family, we had our birth in the work of Martin Luther, it should surprise no one that we came to be called "Lutherans." But that term was originally a nickname and probably should still be so regarded. The name by which Luther's followers were first known— and still are in much of Europe—is "Evangelical," which means "of the gospel."

Luther emphatically did *not* want a church named after him. He said his followers were *catholic* Christians with an *evangelical* emphasis. Thus "Evangelical Catholic" might be the best name for us: it would convey that we are part of the church universal ("catholic") with a gospel orientation ("evangelical"). Many parts of the Lutheran family around the world do not use the word *Lutheran* at all in their official church name. The national churches in certain Scandinavian countries, for example, keep it simple:

Church of Norway
Church of Sweden
National Church of Iceland

There are also churches where the modifier is *Evangelical*, and *Lutheran* again is left out of the name. One of these is the Evangelical Church Mekane Yesus, in Ethiopia, which literally means "Gospel Church where Jesus Dwells." Others using *Evangelical* as the sole adjective are:

Evangelical Church of Greifswald (East Germany)
Evangelical Church of Eritrea (Ethiopia)

Many of our family use "Augsburg Confession" as the key to their identity. They are found particularly in Western and Eastern Europe:

Church of the Augsburg Confession of Alsace
    and Lorraine (France)
Evangelical Church of the Augsburg Confession
    in Austria
Evangelical Church of Augsburg Confession in the
    People's Republic of Poland
Evangelical Church of the Augsburg Confession
    in the Socialist Republic of Romania
Evangelical Church of the Augsburg Confession in
    the Socialist Republic of Slovenia (Yugoslavia)
Slovak Evangelical Church of the Augsburg Confession
    in the CSSR (Czechoslovakia)

Then there are Lutheran churches which favor the term *Protestant*:

Protestant Christian Batak Church (Indonesia)
Christian Protestant Church in Indonesia
Protestant Church in Sabah (Malaysia)

There is even one church in the family which carries the identity of another denomination. The Moravian Church in southern Africa, because it accepts the Lutheran confessional documents, is able to be a member church of the Lutheran World Federation and is counted as part of the global Lutheran family.

The geography of global Lutheranism

If you look at the origins of Lutheran churches around the world, four types emerge. First there are the traditional churches of Europe, where the Reformation began. In Germany, the *Landeskirchen* or regional churches became Lutheran as individual states or rulers decided to identify with the Reformation. In Scandinavia, the pattern was for the entire church of each country to switch from Roman Catholic to Lutheran. In both Germany and Scandinavia, these churches retained close connections with government, and in some cases these relationships continue today.

Second, elsewhere in Europe there are smaller Lutheran churches, living alongside Roman Catholic or Reformed (Calvinist) churches which are numerically much stronger, as in Austria, France, Hungary, and Czechoslovakia. These minority churches developed through the spread of the Lutheran Reformation or by the migration of Lutheran populations, as when Germans moved to Romania or Russia.

Third, when European migration to the Americas and elsewhere occurred, beginning in the 18th century, the Lutherans among them established strong churches in such places as Brazil, Canada, the United States, and Australia. These churches typically found themselves in situations of great religious pluralism, and they learned to live and thrive without formal connection to the political orders.

Fourth, Lutheran churches in much of Africa and Asia, and in parts of Latin America as well, are the result of missionary activity launched by the churches in Europe and North America. The first Lutheran missionaries went from Denmark to India in 1706. Today some of these younger churches in the Southern Hemisphere (especially Africa and Papua New Guinea) are the fastest growing and are themselves sharing church workers with other countries.

Lutherans today are found on all continents and in most nations of the world. By far the majority, however, still live in Europe, where the Lutheran Reformation began. The two Germanies alone account for 40% of the family. In Europe overall live three-fourths of the world's Lutherans. One reason for the large membership of some European churches is that in certain countries all persons are registered as members of the state (Lutheran) churches at birth and remain members unless they petition for removal. If the total Lutheran family is divided by regions, the numbers look like this:

Northern Europe (Denmark, Iceland, Norway, Sweden, and Finland)	21,500,000
Western Europe (West Germany, Austria, Belgium, France, Netherlands, Switzerland, United Kingdom)	21,400,000
Eastern Europe (East Germany, Czechoslovakia, Poland, Romania, Soviet Union, Yugoslavia)	8,100,000*
North America (Canada, United States)	8,800,000
Africa	3,900,000
Asia	3,400,000
Latin America and the Caribbean	1,200,000
Australia and the Pacific	700,000
	68,900,000*

*Plus an estimated 300,000 German-speaking Lutherans in central USSR who are not in organized church bodies.[2]

To put it another way, of every eight Lutherans in the world, five live in Northern and Western Europe, one lives in Eastern Europe, one lives in North America, and one lives somewhere in the Southern Hemisphere.

But raw membership figures can be quite misleading. In the state churches of northern Europe, 95% of the population may be born into a Lutheran church, yet only 5%-10% of them have any ongoing relationship with the church. It has been argued that the Lutheran church in the United States and Canada, with its free-church structure and relatively high percentage of member participation from week to week, is in fact "larger" than the Lutheran church in all of Scandinavia and Germany combined.

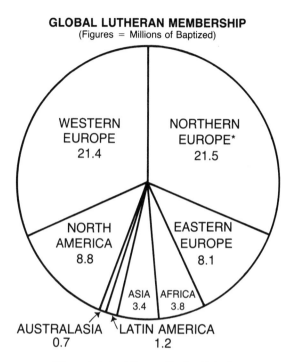

GLOBAL LUTHERAN MEMBERSHIP
(Figures = Millions of Baptized)

WESTERN EUROPE 21.4

NORTHERN EUROPE* 21.5

NORTH AMERICA 8.8

EASTERN EUROPE 8.1

ASIA 3.4

AFRICA 3.8

AUSTRALASIA 0.7

LATIN AMERICA 1.2

*Denmark, Iceland, Norway, Sweden, Finland

Further, there are no doubt more Lutherans in church on a typical Sunday morning in Namibia than in Sweden or Norway or Denmark or Finland, each of which has millions more in nominal Lutheran membership. Certainly the growth in Lutheran membership is greatest in the Southern Hemisphere. The numbers of family members have been increasing especially in Africa, but also in parts of Asia and Latin America. During recent decades the Lutheran total in Europe has been declining and in North America it is resting on a plateau.

The largest churches, counting all who are formally on the roles, are in Europe and North America. The numerical leaders are:

Church of Sweden	7,687,000
Ev. Lutheran Church in Denmark	5,100,000
Ev. Lutheran Church of Finland	4,642,000
Church of Norway	3,850,000
Ev. Lutheran Church of Hannover	
(West Germany)	3,542,000
Lutheran Church in America	3,048,000

If you add the U.S. memberships of the Lutheran Church in America, The American Lutheran Church, and the Association of Evangelical Lutheran Churches (the three groups planning to unite in the late 1980s), the result of 5,400,000 will be the second largest Lutheran church in the world.

Some of the Lutheran populations in Southern Hemisphere nations are becoming sizable, as these figures indicate:

Indonesia	2,231,000
Brazil	1,034,000
India	1,027,000
Tanzania	1,000,000
South Africa	. 704,000
Ethiopia	658,000
Madagascar	600,000
Papua New Guinea	582,000
Namibia	531,000

Namibia, by the way, has a higher percentage of its population in the Lutheran family than any country in the world outside Scandinavia—just over 50%.

The family joins hands

It was not until this century that the Lutheran churches in various parts of the world sought to tie themselves together. Two efforts were made, each following a major war and each motivated in large part by the need to provide postwar relief and rehabilitation. The first led to the founding of the Lutheran World Convention (Eisenach, Germany, 1923). The Convention also met in 1929 (Copenhagen) and 1935 (Paris). It was scheduled to meet next in Philadelphia, but by 1941 Lutherans were once more separated by war. When World War II ended in 1945, a quarter of the world's Lutherans were uprooted and faced with the rebuilding of their lives and their churches. Other Lutherans responded with relief aid, refugee resettlement, and programs of reconstruction.

Then, in 1947, 49 churches from six continents sent representatives to Lund, Sweden, to form the Lutheran World Federation (LWF). Today the LWF includes 99 member churches in 49 countries, representing nearly four-fifths of the world's Lutheran membership.[3]

Of the 14.5 million Lutherans in churches or congregations outside the federation, about 11 million are members of Protestant union churches in Germany. Most of these have not joined the LWF because they are not comfortable with its confessional basis, but they cooperate with the Federation and send observers to its meetings. The major *Lutheran* churches outside the LWF are the Lutheran Church–Missouri Synod (membership of 2.6 million in the United States, 95,000 in Canada) and three others which historically have had ties to the LCMS:

Wisconsin Ev. Lutheran Synod (U.S.)	413,000
Ev. Lutheran Church of Brazil	183,000
Lutheran Church of Australia	117,000

Out of the shambles of World War II, Lutheran churches came together globally. At first it was mainly a cooperative response to war-caused physical need. Soon the Federation became a vehicle for joint work in global mission and evangelism, theological studies and ecumenical commitment (relating to other religious communities), and communication. (See Appendix 4 for an LWF organizational chart.)

Today the work of the LWF is focused in four areas of cooperative activity: World Service, Church Cooperation, Studies, and Communication.

World Service is the largest LWF activity. It is also the world's largest program of material assistance and human development operated by an international religious organization. With resources given by its member churches, national governments, and intergovernmental agencies, LWF World Service is able to provide about $50 million (U.S.) in help annually. Three major activities are carried out by World Service:

● Service programs of World Service include addressing immediate suffering of people anywhere in the world through meeting emergency needs (food, clothing, etc.), rehabilitation, refugee services, and assistance for development. In LWF's earlier years, relief work in postwar Europe and refugee ministry among Palestinians and Hong Kong Chinese were major activities. Palestinians are still receiving help, along with refugees from Angola, Namibia, South Africa, and Burundi. Some 3700 staff persons—all but 90 from the country in which they serve—are currently at work in 17 countries. Much of the giving to Lutheran hunger appeals in North America and Europe is channeled through LWF World Service's refugee and development programs.[4]

● Community Development Service (CDS) helps a particular national church to assist needy people with the basics of life. Projects use local skills, seek to identify with the people, and must serve an entire community, not just Christians. Since 1962 CDS has assisted more than 1000 projects in 46 countries, with funding of more than $100 million in agriculture, education, health care, vocational training, communications, and help for persons with disabilities.

• Research and Social Action is the third basic activity of LWF World Service. This office supports consultations and self-studies within the member churches on the root causes of the widening gap between the world's poor and rich, and engages in development education.

Church Cooperation provides member churches with ways of sharing in order to build up the body of Christ on earth. In the past, the Lutheran church has spread around the world through mission efforts by older churches in Europe and North America. Today, personnel from the younger churches also cross national and cultural boundaries in partnership for mission.

Special funding assists evangelism, in-country scholarships, Christian education, literature, and library programs.

In Eastern Europe, Church Cooperation responds to the special problems of smaller Lutheran churches through established programs and uniquely personal visits.

In Latin America, the need may be to help member churches see their role as members of the ecumenical family. Participation in interchurch programs and study institutions is encouraged.

From Africa come questions on how to set up a pension plan for church workers, how to minister in urban industrial areas, or how to develop a common strategy for theological education.

In Asia, Church Cooperation helps seminaries with common problems.

Since 1981 a youth desk has helped member churches integrate their young people more fully into their life and witness.

Studies is the LWF department which focuses on the theological questions concerning the mission and service of the member churches and the role of LWF as a federation of churches. Without such built-in theological reflection the LWF would lose its center. Within the department the work subdivides into three areas:

• One staff group concentrates on the church as community; for example, studying issues of worship and ministry.

• A second staff group assists the churches through educational services. A worldwide scholarship program provides scholarship or exchange awards to as many as 50 persons each year. A women's desk assists the process of realizing women's rightful place in church and society.

• A third staff group works on Christian witness as related to religious faith, economics, and politics. Member churches are supported in relating to various political ideologies and other world religions.

LWF Studies also cooperates with the Institute for Ecumenical Research in Strasbourg, France. Since 1964 that institute has conducted theological research and interconfessional dialogues for the churches of the federation. Much of its work is done in cooperation with the Commission on Faith and Order of the World Council of Churches.

Communication is the LWF unit which helps member churches with the proclamation of the gospel, especially through modern mass media. Through some 60 projects annually, the churches are helped with broadcasting, publishing, and simpler forms of group communication. The department coordinates regional strategy consultations and training workshops in communication skills.

From the early 1960s until 1977 (when it was seized by the Ethiopian government), the Radio Voice of the Gospel in Addis Ababa transmitted shortwave religion, news, and education programs in many African (and a few Asian) languages.

Lutheran World Information, a weekly news service, is provided in English and German to nearly 4000 recipients around the world; a similar service in French is offered on a less frequent basis. LWF Report/Documentation reaches 5500 church leaders and institutions with major reports and study papers.

Once in seven years

The entire family of LWF member churches comes together, usually every seventh year, in an assembly. The LWF assembly is something like a family reunion. Every member church is entitled to at least one delegate. Advisers, observers, official visitors, and press persons are also present. (In Budapest, Hungary, 1984, nearly 1500 persons were registered; another 15,000 to 20,000 from the Lutheran Church in Hungary participated in one or more of the assembly events.)

The LWF's initial Assembly, at Lund, Sweden, in 1947, was held in the still-tense aftermath of World War II. It was an assembly that brought Lutherans from around the world together in a new federation for cooperative work and witness. But it was also an assembly that reconciled Lutherans who had been on opposite sides of history's bloodiest war.

The 1952 Assembly was held in Hannover, Federal Republic of Germany. It was a joyous time as the German churches welcomed to their soil—the Reformation's heartland—fellow Lutherans from the rest of the world. But it was also a somber time as the churches came to realize that Europe and other parts of the world were being divided politically—and, it seemed, permanently—into East and West.

In 1957 the Assembly went to North America for the first time. In Minneapolis-St. Paul the various sessions and mass rallies attracted some quarter of a million people. Without knowing that Pope John XXIII would soon call

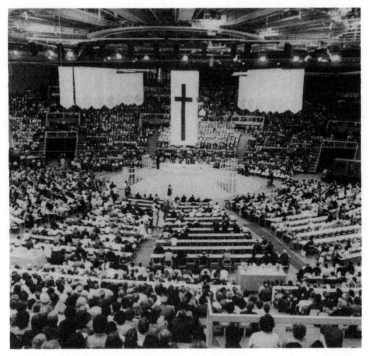

Some 11,000 Hungarians joined 1300 Lutherans from around the world at the opening service of the LWF Seventh Assembly in Budapest.

for a Second Vatican Council, the 1957 Assembly took a big step toward interconfessional dialogue by creating a special commission which, several years later, would become the Institute for Ecumenical Research in Strasbourg.

In 1963 the Assembly returned to Europe, meeting in Finland's capital, Helsinki. This Assembly tried to state the doctrine of justification in modern terms. It was also an assembly at which delegations from the younger churches of Asia, Africa, and Latin America raised significant social, economic, and political questions.

LWF had hoped to have its Fifth Assembly in East Germany in 1969, but government coolness to the idea led

to rescheduling it for 1970 in Brazil. Pôrto Alegre was to
be the location, but just weeks before the first assembly
in the Southern Hemisphere was to open there was another switch. Several churches announced they would
protest political oppression in Brazil by not sending representatives. The Assembly was moved to Evian, France,
near the LWF's Geneva headquarters. That meeting was
marked by the strong participation of youth and by their
joining with other delegates to press the Federation and
its member churches to address matters of international
justice.

Finally, in 1977, the LWF did hold an assembly in a
country of the South. The locale was Dar es Salaam, Tanzania. Dr. Carl Mau Jr., general secretary of the LWF since
1974, later said, "We were influenced by the place, the
hunger, poverty, injustice and oppression facing us everywhere. We were also influenced by the vitality of the host
church that surrounded us with remarkable singing and
worship." Meeting on the African continent, the LWF for
the first time elected as president a leader from the South.[5]
It also took the historic action of declaring the apartheid
system of South Africa to be inconsistent with Lutheran
understanding of the biblical faith.

The latest Assembly—Budapest, 1984—was the first to
be held in Eastern Europe. It marked the first election to
the LWF presidency of a leader from a church living in a
Marxist society. The Budapest gathering also followed the
Dar es Salaam action on apartheid by declaring that two
white churches in southern Africa had removed themselves from fellowship with other members of the federation by refusing to condemn apartheid and to move
toward full partnership with the black churches which are
their neighbors. (A complete discussion of this action appears in Chapter 5.)

The LWF's Eighth Assembly will likely be held in 1990
or 1991, although some voices at Budapest predicted the

world as we know it would not last that long unless the nations find a way to control the nuclear threat. As they proclaim the gospel, with its clear implications for a world of peace with justice, the churches of the Lutheran family see a role for themselves in helping to prevent nuclear catastrophe (see Chapter 8). It is a major element in the hope for the world which these churches find in Christ.

Words to ponder

"It is also taught among us that such faith should produce good fruits and good works and that we must do all such good works as God has commanded, but we should do them for God's sake and not place our trust in them as if thereby to merit favor before God."

—Augsburg Confession 6

"How silly that expression was that for centuries we believed hit the nail on the head: 'To lead a good life, one must be a Lutheran; to die a good death, one must be a Catholic.' Anyone who follows Luther will live well and die even better, for at the end of the dark tunnel stands Someone who loves us and to whom we can look forward. That is Luther's ecumenical legacy, for which we should give him thanks."

> —Peter Manns, Roman Catholic priest and scholar, in his book *Martin Luther* (New York: Crossroad, 1983)

"Christians should cross out the word 'hopeless' in their dictionaries because of their faith in Christ. Instead we should draw pictures of hope. Like Martin Luther we should 'plant apple trees' even when we know the day of judgment is near."

> —Pastor Annette Nuber, Federal Republic of Germany, in sermon at concluding worship of the Budapest Assembly

"The Lutheran World Federation has never made membership in the Federation a criterion for help, support, or involvement in the work and life of the federation. In that sense the LWF has sought to serve the whole Lutheran communion. In that sense it has understood its tasks to cultivate faith and confession among all Lutheran churches of the world."

> —Carl H. Mau Jr., LWF general secretary, in address to Budapest Assembly

For discussion

1. Read the quotations at the start and end of the chapter, reflect on them, and share comments or questions about them.

2. Does the group agree that Lutherans are yearning for reunion with other Christians? Does the group think that Lutherans ought to pursue the goal of church unity? If so, how?

3. Would you be comfortable with a name other than *Lutheran* for your church? What possible names would you consider?

4. Do you know of activities of the Lutheran World Federation which touch the life of your congregation? Activities your congregation supports through LWF? Make a list of them. Share with your church council and congregation.

5. What would your non-Lutheran friends mention as *uniquely* characteristic of the Lutheran church? Ask three of them this question during the coming week and share the responses when the discussion group reconvenes.

Members of the Hungarian Lutheran Church worshiped with Assembly participants at several services.

2

What Gives the Family Hope?

"O Israel, hope in the Lord! For with the Lord there is steadfast love, and with him is plenteous redemption."
—*Psalm 130:7*

"Hope is the refusal to accept the reading of reality which is the majority opinion, and one does that only at great political and existential risk. On the other hand, hope is subversive for it limits the grandiose pretension of the present."
—*Walter Brueggemann,* The Prophetic Imagination *(Philadelphia: Fortress, 1978), p. 67*

Christians are people who should "abound in hope." So wrote St. Paul in his letter to the Romans (15:13). Why should we hope? What are the reasons for the hope that is in us? And what is the content of that hope?

"In Christ—Hope for the World" was the theme for the Seventh Assembly of the Lutheran World Federation (Budapest, 1984). Does that theme have anything to say to us? Does it hold any hope for us in a day when the fears of human beings are probably as intense—and for good reason—as they have ever been?

The Lutheran family in Christ has always placed its hope in the resurrection of Christ. We share that hope with other

Christians, of course, who would no doubt agree with the writer of 1 Peter:

> Blessed be the God and Father of our Lord Jesus Christ! By his great mercy we have been born anew to a living hope through the resurrection of Jesus Christ from the dead (1:3).

However, Lutherans have given special attention to certain theological themes. A brief review of three of them would be in order.

Reasons for our hope

1. *We have hope because we are justified by grace.* Lutherans see God's activity in loving human beings, despite our repeated rejection of God, as the basic biblical message. In making us, sustaining us with life, forgiving us as we rebel, redeeming us through the life, death, and resurrection of Christ—in all of this God shows love toward us, love we in no way deserve. And that's what grace means: unearned love, freely given. It is also part of Lutheran understanding that we appropriate this gift of God's love by faith—not by behaving in a certain way but by believing that it is so. And even the ability to believe is a gift of God's Spirit.

2. *We have hope because of the meaning of the cross of Christ.* The cross is God's way of saying that we human beings are not left alone. God comes to be with us, precisely in our suffering, our despairing, our dying. God identifies with us all by eating and drinking with the rejected ones, by standing with "the least" among us, by hanging with criminals condemned to death. While Easter and its empty tomb remind us of God's victory in which we share, Good Friday and the cross remind us of the lengths to which God is willing to go in being fully with us in our human despair—and even in our death. Because of the cross and the empty tomb together, we have hope. And that hope

is quite different from optimism. Whereas optimism is based on human factors such as politics or sociology, hope depends on God's purposes and faithfulness. The cross helps us at the same time to live with human pessimism and to be surpassingly hopeful about what God is doing in the world.

3. *We have hope because we have direct access to God.* Lutherans have insisted that *all* believers are priests before God, that none of us needs to have that relationship mediated through any other human being. Lutherans didn't eliminate clergy (as did some later Protestant movements), but we have tried to redefine their role. We see our pastors as people who are trained and called apart (ordained) for the ministry of leadership in the church—especially preaching and teaching the gospel, presiding at public worship, and exemplifying a life of service to God and neighbor. Baptism ushers us into God's family, and all Christians have the same standing in that family. All are in the universal priesthood of believers. And because of that we have hope.

These are historic Lutheran theological themes. They've been part of our family tradition since the early 16th century. Added to them for many in the Lutheran family today is another:

We have hope because God promises liberation from all that oppresses us. Our strong grounding in the Scriptures has led many Lutherans to find hope in the biblical word that God is setting at liberty those who are captive to human structures that enslave. This hope focuses not just on salvation in the hereafter but also in the present age. We have hope because of God's activity not just in the past and the future but also in the present. As signs of God's promise, we look not just to the cross but also to the exodus. Hope of this sort has grown as a theme among

Lutherans in recent times, and the past three LWF assemblies, especially, have reflected the new importance of that theme.

So what do Lutherans say about hope when they gather together in the late 20th century? What did they do with hope at Budapest in 1984?

A biblical theme

First, there was the reminder that hope is a central theme of the Bible. Two years earlier, LWF President Josiah Kibira had spoken about that:

> We have chosen for our theme "In Christ: Hope for the World." I do not think it is only in Tanzania that there is much pessimism and questioning as to what the near future might hold. . . . At this time the word "hope" is very appropriate. And it is indeed a great Christian concept, more central to the Bible than we might have known up to now. We have so long talked about *love* and *faith.* In order that these words may remain and grow within us and within the churches, we now need to receive much more *hope.* We know that our Savior Jesus Christ is its real source.[1]

The emphasis on hope is especially clear in the letters of the New Testament, where it is regularly grounded in the resurrection of Christ. But St. Paul indicates (Rom. 15:4) that the Hebrew Scriptures also, before the time of Christ, were written to provide hope:

> For whatever was written in former days was written for our instruction, that by steadfastness and by the encouragement of the scriptures we might have hope.

At the Assembly in Budapest there was much talk about the loss of hope among most people in today's world. In the face of that death of hope, what can the church dare to speak? The church has but two choices, said Klaus-Peter Hertzsch, a theologian from the German Democratic

Republic, in his keynote address: either to preach the good news or to admit it has become redundant and has nothing distinctive to say. The church has but one thing to say: *In Christ, there is good news. God loves us and will not abandon us.*

Dr. Hertzsch spoke of the biblical pictures of hope as the answer to the world's present shortage of hope-filled images. He mentioned the pictures of paradise and the promised land, of arrival at the parental home, of God's shalom and the messianic age, of Jesus' parables of the kingdom, of the vision of the heavenly Jerusalem and of the one who will wipe away all tears from our eyes. To appreciate these pictures we all must return to the kind of expectation we experienced when we were children. As adults, we think we know reality and thus have a hard time envisioning something new, but:

> With children it is different. We get up in the morning with the hope that something quite beautiful will happen to us today, something quite unexpected, some quite new experience. As adults . . . we tend to think . . . that we are already familiar with reality in all its forms and can therefore only really hope for what others have already experienced at one time or another. Children . . . know very well how unfamiliar they are with the real world. Their hope, therefore, is far more radical and rich. It is hope for what is still quite unknown to them, of which only in retrospect can it be said, "I would never even have dreamt of that"; hope of the utterly and completely unexpected and surprising, of the overwhelming that surpasses everything familiar and known. Jesus said, "Whoever does not receive the kingdom of God like a child shall not enter it" (Mark 10:15). But kingdom of God means hope.[2]

The word *hope* is ambiguous. In English and other languages as well the word means at the same time the activity of hoping and that which is hoped for. Thus we can say that we are "born anew to a living hope through the resurrection of Jesus Christ" (1 Peter 1:3)—energized anew in hope. And we can also say that God is the "hope of Israel, its savior in time of trouble" (Jer. 14:8)—God is the *content* of our hope. God's actions give us reason to hope—and it is God, coming among us to fulfill the kingdom, in whom we hope.

Hope for the creation

At Budapest the theme of hope was developed through three subthemes: hope for creation, hope for humankind, and hope for the church. In his major presentation on the first of these, Dr. Emmanuel Abraham, leader of Ethiopia's Mekane Yesus Church, expressed deep distress over the ways human beings have exploited God's earth and one another. But he also spoke of his belief that God's purposes will prevail and that the gospel is good news also for the creation:

> Whatever men and women may think or do, the Lord God has worked and is working to bring about his eternal purpose for his creation. . . . It is my belief that the light of the gospel of Christ will continue to shine on this earth and that his church will strive to hold him up as the only hope for this world, while endeavoring to care for his creation with love that reflects his unspeakable love.

In adopting a statement on "Caring for God's Endangered Creation," the Assembly proposed that Lutherans confess their failure to witness adequately to the First Article of the Creed "in a way that would have illuminated the danger to God's creation." The assembly also urged that the LWF give program attention to care of the creation in several ways, including:

- urging member churches and their congregations to proclaim God's goodness in creating and continuing to care

for the world, and God's redemption in Christ as embracing the totality of that creation (Rom. 8:21-25);
- providing resources, consultation services, and other support for educational efforts throughout the member churches in a form relevant to local situations;
- requesting the United Nations to declare a "Year of Ecology";
- asking congregations and church members to focus their consumption practices toward greater conservation of natural resources;
- developing, in cooperation with the World Council of Churches and other agencies, a major study program on the relationship between science and theology as they touch ecology and ethics.

As the biblical writers viewed it, creation has had to bear the burden of a fallen humanity's greedy and exploitive behavior. But in the same breath the Bible tells us that the entire creation will benefit when humanity is set free from its bondage (Romans 8, Colossians 1). There will be not only a new heaven, but also a new earth, and God will dwell in both. And so the Hebrew Scriptures admonished the

> earth and sky, sea and fields and everything in them to be glad at the prospect of what is to come (Psalm 96:11-12). The trees in the woods will shout for joy, the rivers will clap their hands, and the hills will sing together with joy before the Lord (Psalm 98:7-8).[3]

Hope for humankind

Can an international gathering engender hope because of the *place* in which it is held? The Budapest location for this Lutheran family reunion led many to think so. In an announcement of a youth gathering held prior to the Assembly, Peter Lodberg and Tamas Fabiny wrote (December 1983): "We come to Budapest because we want to experience and express unity, in spite of all the tensions

and diversities we know from our particular political, social, and ecclesiastical backgrounds."

Not only the pre-Assembly youth gathering, but also
the Assembly itself fulfilled that hope. Participants lived
and celebrated the unity in Christ that is stronger and
deeper than the divisions the human family knows. The
"Message of the Assembly," adopted at its close, expresses
that discovery in this paragraph:

> We saw a sign of that hope in our coming together from
> all parts of the world as Lutherans who share in a common
> confession of faith in Christ. Meeting in Budapest, Hungary,
> the Federation was assembling for the first time in a socialist
> country in Eastern Europe. Our gathering here and the
> hospitality we received here showed us that in the church
> of Christ we can have confidence in each other and can
> build bridges between people across political and ideolog-
> ical boundaries.[4]

The fact that the world Lutheran family had chosen to
meet in Eastern Europe gave affirmation and hope to the
churches of those countries, especially. The reason for their
joy was rooted, of course, in the reality that one of the
deep divisions in the human family today is the one sep-
arating West from East, and this meeting seemed able to
transcend that division.

But the East-West division is not the only chasm facing
humankind. We are also divided between rich and poor.
There are tensions between races, between women and
men, between generations.

What hope for healing of these human divisions is there
in Christ? Or does Christ symbolize just one more such
division, that between those who follow him and those
who do not?

Christians do not have a totally admirable record on
history's scorecard for healing human divisions. The followers of Jesus, Lutherans among them, have not always
led the rest of humanity on the paths to ending wars and

violence, to closing the gap between rich and poor, to giving full equality and participation to women, to honoring the contributions of the very young and the very old.

Yet overall, Christianity in history has been a strong, often decisive, force for justice, for peace, for women, for the poor. And when Christians have failed it is not the gospel that was lacking. What failed was our understanding of its meaning for healing humanity, and our will to translate that meaning into concrete social and political realities. We have too often individualized or spiritualized the gospel's message, relating it only to some private, interior, or otherworldly reality.

Those gathered in the Marxist-Leninist setting of Budapest in 1984 were reminded that the church exists in the world to be a tool of reconciliation, not just between humanity and God, but also among human beings themselves. And so they turned again to the New Testament reminders of what has, indeed, happened in Christ:

● Differences such as nationality, economic station, and gender can no longer be used to justify separation or supremacy. "So there is no difference between Jews and Gentiles, between slaves and free men, between men and women; you are all one in union with Christ Jesus" (Gal. 3:28 TEV).

● Because of Christ's sacrifice on the cross, humanity is now to be viewed as *one*. "For Christ himself has brought us peace by making Jews and Gentiles one people. With his own body he broke down the wall that separated them and kept them enemies. . . . in order to create out of the two races one new people in union with himself, in this way making peace" (Eph. 2:14-15 TEV).

● We who know Christ are charged with extending his reconciling work. "All this is from God, who through Christ reconciled us to himself and gave us the ministry of reconciliation" (2 Cor. 5:18).

Youth presented their concerns to the Assembly with the help of song and dance.

Some of the specifics of our call to be reconcilers in a suffering world will be highlighted later, especially in Chapters 6, 7, and 8. For now it is enough to say, in the words of the Assembly Study Book:

> Christ is our hope because he has already remedied what was fundamentally wrong with humankind. He also real-istically portrayed Christian life in an alien world. His entire ministry . . . serves as an illustration. John describes how we have come to know love through Christ's death for us, how we are called to walk in his footsteps, and love even enemies as he loved us.[5]

Hope for the church

If the church is to be the carrier of such a message, won't the church itself need to be renewed?

Yes! And the hope we have in Christ also gives us reason to hope for that renewal.

The world needs and wants badly a message of hope today. But when it looks to our churches, does the world see or hear anything new, anything different, anything hopeful? Does the world find in us salt and light?

> Those who still practice a religion are not manifestly different from those who don't. The religious are themselves secularized, since they have turned their attention away from the mysteries, myth, magic and miracle, and to the things of this world, getting a new kitchen for the church, organizing a bowling team to compete in the church league, a reading group to discuss current fiction, or a sensitivity group so people can find out who they really are.[6]

But what question is the world asking for which the church, with the gospel, may have an answer? In Luther's time—at least for Luther and many others of his generation who responded to his teaching—the question clearly was: How can I find a gracious God?

At the 1963 Assembly of the LWF in Helsinki, it was said that the world's question had become more elementary: God, where are you?

Today the question seems to be neither of these, but rather: It's not important to me if there's a God, but can you help me learn how to live with my neighbor?

Now the gospel includes an answer to the question of how we find neighbors who are gracious. It is essentially that, in Christ, we find the motivation and the power to *become* a gracious neighbor. But the church's problem may be that we do not take the time to learn what questions the world is asking before we rush in with our answers, often answers that met an earlier day's questions. It is true, as has been said, that preparation for effective proclamation of the gospel will always require that the proclaimer have the Bible on one knee and today's newspaper on the other. Our proclamation does not always speak to the needs people are experiencing—and that includes those who are members of the churches as well as those who are not.

> We tend to give too many answers, too soon, in set axioms, without involving the people to whom we intend to address the answer. The people we are addressing appear to tell us that Christians may have the right answer but they are not able to relate it to the questions in their minds. . . . We must not impose upon others our definitions of their needs.[7]

Another impediment to our witness is the style of life led by the church, especially in countries where it has enjoyed wealth and worldly power. The church's life preaches sermons that are more powerful than words:

- Does our quest for affluence and comfort in our buildings deny our words about the gospel as good news to the poor?
- Does our style of governance and leadership recognize the gifts of all—women and men, old and young, ordained and nonordained, able-bodied and those with disabilities?
- Does the fellowship of the congregation reflect the composition of the community in which it lives— in economic class, racial background, and other ways?
- Are the resources of the congregation, including its property, available to benefit those who are not members?
- Is the financial giving of the faithful used almost exclusively for ministries which serve those who give?
- Are the members equipped only for building up the church as an organization, or are they enabled to become

witnesses at their places of work, in their neighborhoods, and through their citizenship in the political order?

In Christ, there is hope also for the church. But only if we can learn to live as though the church is not an ultimate, not an end in itself, but an instrument God would use to bless us who are part of it and, through us (perhaps despite us), to bless the whole world.

> The church is a tool in God's hand, an instrument of God's will in this world—which will not be needed in the same way when God one day fulfills his promises. For the church, hope is that it may succeed in its task; it has been chosen for a divine purpose. Without Christ's promise to be with the church always, preserving and sustaining it as his own body, this would be meaningless. Only in Christ is there hope for the church. The gift of the gospel, the Word of God that justifies sinners and grants them new life, is forever valid for the church. Provided it preaches and serves the authentic gospel, the church is promised that the "gates of hell" will not overcome it. Through its existence and in its mission it warrants a well-founded hope also for the future of the world.[8]

Words to ponder

"You must, of course, continue faithful on firm foundation, and must not allow yourselves to be shaken from the hope you gained when you heard the gospel."
> —Colossians 1:23 TEV

"I have often been asked: 'What is the greatest difficulty you face in moving from India to England?' I have always answered: 'The disappearance of hope.' . . . Even in the most squalid slums of Madras there was always the belief that things could be improved. . . . In England, by contrast, it is hard to find any such hope. Apart from those whose lives are shaped by the Christian hope founded on the resurrection of Christ as the pledge of a new creation, there is little sign among the citizens of this country of the sort of confidence in the future which was certainly present in the earlier years of this century."

> —Leslie Newbigin, British theologian, after nearly 40 years of missionary service in India, in *The Other Side of 1984* (Geneva: Risk Books [World Council of Churches], 1983)

"If I knew the world were to end tomorrow, I would still plant an apple tree today."
> —attributed to Martin Luther

"The church is not dead, though it could be argued that it is mortally sick. It is Hope that has died; not dramatically, not with an audible death-rattle, but imperceptibly as though some malevolent force has slowly but surely turned down the wick of the lamp of Faith."
> —Colin Morris, *The Hammer of the Lord*

"Every assembly of the Lutheran World Federation, including this Seventh Assembly, could be its last. Every year of human history, even this year 1984, could be the last. In principle and theoretically, we have always known this, even if we have never hesitated to fill up our diaries a year ahead with engagements. Today, however, it no longer seems quite so theoretical. It suddenly confronts us directly—an ending brought about, moreover, by humanity itself."

> —Klaus-Peter Hertzsch, theologian from the University of Jena, German Democratic Republic, in keynote address at Budapest Assembly of LWF

"My hope is built on nothing less than Jesus' blood and righteousness; No merit of my own I claim, but wholly lean on Jesus' name. On Christ the solid rock I stand; all other ground is sinking sand."

> —refrain from hymn by Edward Mote
> (1787-1874)

"What oxygen is for the lungs, hope is for human existence—the store of hope determines the fate of humankind."

> —Emil Brunner, theologian, in his book *Das Ewige als Zukunft und Gegenwart* (The Eternal as Future and Present), 1965

For discussion

1. Read the quotations at chapter's start and end, reflect on them, and share comments or questions about them.

2. St. Paul writes in 1 Corinthians 13 that "faith, hope, and love abide . . . but the greatest of these is love." What is the significance of his statement that faith and hope take second place to love?

3. Do you agree with Dr. Hertzsch that adults lose the ability to expect the unexpected? If he is correct, how can we recover the child within us—the childlike trust in the gospel—as we hope?

4. Discuss examples of contributions by Christians to healing human divisions (war/peace, rich/poor, racial enmity, women/men, young/old, etc.). Then discuss examples of healing that remains to be done—and the role Christians could play in those tasks.

5. Discuss the "sermons" preached to the world—without words—by your congregation; by the church in regional, national, and international expressions; by us who are Christians in our daily lives.

6. Walk through this next week conscious of what gives you *hope* to keep going. Do ideas or feelings play the greater role? Celebrate sources of hope you encounter during the week. Discuss with your family or friends over a meal.

Pastors from other parts of the world took part in Communion liturgies in Hungarian Lutheran congregations during the Seventh Assembly's community visits.

3

What Is the Family's Task?

"We stand in awe as the missio dei *[mission of God] is again facilitated by the scattering of the nations. People who are locked into one cultural understanding become confronted with migrating people from all over the world."*

> —Margaret Wold of the United States, in her presentation on mission at the LWF Seventh Assembly

"Lutheran churches have a long history of involvement [with poor people] through diaconic and development activities and more recently also through advocacy for economic and social justice. At the same time, Lutheran churches often tend to identify themselves with the middle class and its values, and the poor have little place in—or influence on—their life and witness."

> —"Working Paper on Mission," received by LWF Seventh Assembly (see note 2 in this chapter)

We members of the Lutheran family, in our daily lives, do just about everything imaginable. We are sent into the world to love our neighbor. One way we do this is by working in a variety of occupations, providing services or products which will help our neighbor to live. In so doing, we serve God, our neighbor, and, of course, ourselves.

But we also serve in the everyday world by fulfilling several other roles: citizen of political entities, payer of taxes, consumer of services and goods, contributor or recipient of voluntary serving, member of a particular family. In all these roles we have callings to fulfill and we seek to do so faithfully. These are primary tasks of members in the family of believers. We would prefer to carry them out with encouragement and nurture and counsel from the larger believing community, the church. But most of us today must find our way in fulfilling our various worldly callings as scattered individuals. When we undertake these tasks of our daily existence, we are, whether we think about it or not, the church *scattered*.

The church *gathered* also has its task, its assignment. We have work to do as the collective body of believers. Part of that work, clearly, is to help equip and enable us all for our work in the world as persons trying to love God by serving our neighbor. Another part of the church's task is our corporate activity as the people of God—those things we do together *as church*, for the sake of the world. We normally call such activity our *mission*, that to which we are sent by God—the proclamation of the gospel through words and actions. The *communication* of God's message and the church's work is a part of our mission task. Further, as the gathered family of God we *worship* God, celebrating God's gifts to us and exploring the needs of the whole world in the light of God's word and will.

Each of these aspects of the church's task—*education* for our work in the world, *mission, communication,* and *worship*—received major attention at the Lutheran World Federation's 1984 Assembly. All four will be explored in this chapter.

Ministry by all the baptized

Assembly delegates received and transmitted to the LWF Department of Studies for consideration a brief reflection on the equipping of all baptized persons for ministry. Among the points made are these:

1. There is but one ministry of Jesus Christ and all believers are ordained into it by baptism.

2. Our baptism marks us with the cross, which requires that we be bearers of the cross, that is, servants to other people.

3. While there is one ministry, it has various expressions. The tasks of clergy and the rest of the people of God are a partnership—interdependent, mutual, reciprocal. Clergy are not to maintain control in the church and the laity must move out of passivity and apathy.

4. The study of the Bible equips us for our ministry in the ordinary world, not for sitting in church pews.

5. Theological education must be suited to the actual needs of believers, which means exploring new models of structuring and locating seminary training to move it closer to the congregations.

The Assembly also referred several recommendations to the LWF Executive Committee for consideration, including requests that the LWF support and assist the member churches by:

• increasing its help to theological education in Asia, Africa, and Latin America, with a priority on doing such education in the settings where ministry is to be done;

• encouraging exchange of teachers and other church personnel from South to North as well as from North to South;

• urging member churches to make educational opportunities available to women and men on a basis of complete equality;

• developing educational helps to assist the churches with creation of ecumenical awareness, especially at the local level;

• sponsoring a study on the role of informal learning in the parish, including education of congregational leaders and pastors in social psychology, communication theory, and group dynamics;

- giving attention to the LWF assembly itself as an educational process when evaluating the seventh and planning the eighth.

People with disabling conditions

As a result of action taken by the Budapest Assembly, serious attention will be given to ministries with persons who have disabling conditions. The report of the working group on enabling ministry included comments on "Participation of People with Disabling Conditions." The paper states there are 500 million persons in the world with physical or mental disabilities of chronic or permanent nature, 80% of them in the low-income countries. The paper argues that disablement is less a physical problem than a psycho-social one.

Disabled people are not so much our problem; rather we, the not-yet-disabled people, are their *problem.*[1]

The statement argues that the society and congregation need disabled persons every bit as much as disabled persons need the society and congregation. Each needs the other for wholeness. These recommendations were adopted by the Assembly for executive committee consideration:

1. that preparations for the next Assembly be intentional in the selection of persons with disabilities as delegates, since such persons bring both gifts and challenges that are unique to the ministry of Christians;

2. that planning for the next Assembly give more consideration to physical arrangements that would not prevent participation by disabled persons;

3. that an LWF staff position to facilitate participation of persons with disabilities be considered, such a desk to

provide various helps to the member churches and to the LWF.

It was the first time in the history of the LWF that a special focus was given to the study of ministry with persons who have disabilities. A 20-minute drama presented to the Assembly depicted typical relationships in which persons with disabilities are consciously or unconsciously segregated socially. A Christ-figure was shown as the first to embrace those with disabilities, breaking down social barriers and drawing all participants into a new community in Christ.

Mission: guidelines for joint action

A new "Working Paper on Mission," received by the LWF Assembly in Budapest and transmitted for study in the member churches, describes mission in this way:

> Mission is the proclamation of the Gospel in word and deed, in which grace is the determinative factor. . . . The character of Christian mission is therefore determined by two fundamental themes:
>
> > Mission is the ongoing saving work of God the Father, Son, and Holy Spirit.
> >
> > Mission is God's mandate to his people to participate in his continuing saving work.
>
> . . . Mission, in other words, belongs to the very being of the church. Consequently, participation in mission is the task of every Christian individual through baptism, the task of every local congregation to nurture and equip its members for mission, and the common task of all churches.[2]

The Assembly stated with the utmost clarity that the primary task of the family of God is mission. Education and nurture in the faith are means to the end, which is mission. Evangelical and diaconal service in development and public advocacy are all part of mission. Worship is the celebration of opportunities for mission and the praise of the God who calls us into mission. Mission is the most complete way, then, to speak of the family's work or task. It is what we are about and will not end until the kingdom of God comes in its fullness.

It is thus no surprise that one of the major actions of the Budapest Assembly was the adoption of "LWF Guidelines for Joint Action in Mission." Because of the importance of these 12 criteria for the interdependent activity of Lutheran churches in their shared global mission, we reproduce them here as a basis for reflection and discussion:

LWF Guidelines for Joint Action in Mission

The urgency of the missionary task, in the present context and on all continents, calls the churches to intensify their own mission efforts as well as their joint action in mission.

1. There are two general guidelines for all joint action. . ..
- Mission is the common responsibility of every Christian, every congregation, and every church.
- Mission in each place is the privilege and common responsibility of the worldwide church.

2. The primary responsibility for responding to mission challenges in a given area rests with the local church or churches, acting on behalf of the church universal. . . .

3. Each church's experiences, insights, theological heritage, and personnel and financial resources are gifts from God for the mission of the whole church. They therefore cannot be considered as its sole possessions but are to be shared. . . .

4. If the local church does not have sufficient resources for responding to its mission challenges, it shall seek cooperation with neighboring churches as well as with other churches that can contribute complementary experiences and insights.

5. Acknowledging Jesus Christ as Lord and Savior, every joint action in mission is to be designed to manifest the unity of the church across ethnic, social, and cultural boundaries, and should also reflect the different cultural backgrounds and social contexts of the people for whom missionary proclamation is intended.

6. Joint actions should be directed toward the whole human being, seeking close linkage between the evangelistic and service arms of the church(es) in ways best suited within each context.

7. Every church involved in joint actions in mission is to assure its share of financing such actions.

8. The funding level of joint mission projects should be in proportion to the standard of living in the area and in line with the available material resources of the local church(es).

9. While all participating churches shall be involved in the planning and decision for joint action for mission, the local church in the area concerned shall also be fully involved in such activity from the very beginning.

10. If a church is not aware of its mission responsibilities or opportunities, churches both nearby and in other areas of the world should initiate conversations with that church, encourage it to accept the challenges at hand, and offer advice and assistance as necessary.

11. If joint actions are planned in areas where no local church exists, churches from closely related areas should be involved.

12. The LWF is to assist its member churches in meeting a particular mission challenge in a variety of ways, depending on the scope of the challenge and according to its mandate:

a. In cases of local mission challenges, the initiative and action are the mandate of the local member church(es) where such exist. It or they can then turn to the LWF for help. Requests will be considered by the LWF according to its appropriate procedures. The interrelatedness of evangelism and service should be reflected in close cooperation between the Departments of Church Cooperation and World Service.

b. In cases of mission challenges related to several countries, the LWF *may* act as a facilitator or coordinator for member churches of the area concerned and it may initiate joint actions in mission if asked by a member church.

c. In cases of global mission challenges, the LWF *shall* through its appropriate organs plan and propose to its member churches joint mission projects and, when necessary, carry pilot programs on their behalf and with their cooperation.

d. In cases of mission challenges in areas where there are no member churches, the LWF may, when one or more of its member churches elsewhere so request, initiate joint actions in mission and invite churches to cooperate in them, provided churches in neighboring areas are prepared to participate.

What does it mean that the member churches of the LWF have adopted these guidelines? They say four significant things to us:

1. Every Christian, every congregation, every church body is responsible for mission.

2. We're in mission *together* as a Lutheran family around the world and no church can act unilaterally. We enter and maintain mission activity through challenging each other, consulting each other, and supporting each other.

3. The resources for personnel, theological insights, money, and other gifts provided by God for each member church to manage do not belong to that church alone; all the rest of the family has a rightful claim on them because they are given by God for the use of the whole church.

4. The role of the Lutheran World Federation is to coordinate, communicate, stimulate, and (when necessary) instigate.

One element not included in the guidelines is the ecumenical—how do Lutheran churches in mission work with the rest of the Christian family? The Budapest Assembly gave much attention to world Lutheranism's ecumenical relationships—both in general (see Chapter 4) and in the "Working Paper on Mission"—but basically ignored it in the joint action for mission proposals. The omission is an unfortunate one.

Mission: the current context

The Assembly also adopted a set of recommendations for consideration by the LWF Executive Committee pertaining to mission in the context of secularization/modernization and amid the challenge of world faiths such as Islam, Hinduism, Buddhism, and newer religious movements. Among the recommendations are these:

1. The LWF should stimulate joint actions in mission by member churches in relation to:

- urban settings
- migrant people
- education for mission (both pastors and members generally)
- secularized settings (e.g. scientific community, peace research centers, industrialists and trade union leaders)
- the challenge of other faiths
- youth and university students

In all these areas, special consideration needs to be given to the place of the poor in mission understanding.

2. The LWF should engage member churches in dialog concerning occupational groups with a high degree of geographic mobility, such as seafarers, students, commercial representatives, diplomatic and development workers, flight personnel, truckers, migrant workers, and military personnel.

3. The LWF should urge member churches to give a higher priority to study of and contact with other faith communities, and should offer LWF help to that end, with special attention to Islam.

4. The LWF should study the question of mixed marriages between Christians and people of other faiths.

5. The LWF should continue its study of yoga and meditation and should urge member churches to intensify their study of and response to forms of spirituality offered by newer religious movements.

6. The LWF and the churches should "find ways and means to mobilize Christian youth to assist and witness to youth at critical frontiers of mission, such as new religious movements."

The Assembly also noted and commended special LWF studies that are under way on primal religion in Africa, the challenge of Islam, and the theology of religions.

Communication, the gospel, and culture

The church's central task is one of communication: spreading the message of the gospel. The church also needs to see that new developments in communication technology are changing people by changing the cultures in which we live. For both reasons, said the Budapest Assembly, Lutherans should give more thoughtful attention to what has been labeled "The New Information Age." The Assembly adopted these recommendations pertaining to communication:

1. All member churches should take seriously the challenge of the New Information Age and LWF Department of Communication is expected to support them with study material.

2. While it is recognized that the gospel is best communicated person-to-person, member churches are urged to equip their congregations with an understanding of

communication and media, to help church members to become discriminating in their listening and viewing, to train Christians for professional service in public media, and to integrate the church communication operations more fully into their total ministry.

3. Member churches are encouraged to study carefully the documents of the New World Information and Communication Order (from the United Nations), and to use as a guide the World Association of Christian Communication statement, "New World Information and Communication Order: a Christian Perspective."[3] (NWICO has sought to focus an international debate on inequities in global communication: the control of media and news services largely in the North, the cultural degradation of the South, and the search for new communication structures that are not viewed by the poor as oppressive. The churches have not been much involved in the debate, and the Assembly thus urged Lutherans to give attention to these issues.)

4. The LWF should consider reopening a communication research desk and, in planning the Eighth Assembly, should take communication principles seriously and include on the program a major presentation on communication.

Worship: sign of hope for the world

When Christians gather to worship in the name of the triune God, the world receives a sign of hope. That hope, said the LWF Assembly, resides in the living Christ, who is present in Word and sacraments.

The Assembly report on worship notes that Christian worship is an activity requiring continued shaping and tailoring to the specific situation and need of every community of believers. The LWF Department of Studies was thanked for its assistance to the member churches in the area of worship. Its work on *Laudamus* (5th ed.), the LWF collection of hymns and liturgies newly issued for the Budapest Assembly, was noted, and its document, "Worship Among Lutherans," was commended to the churches.[4]

The Assembly asked the LWF Executive Committee to give consideration for the next years to a set of tasks related to worship, including:

1. How to make the Sunday service the integrative force of the congregation, as its "plenary assembly."[5]

2. How to affirm "the central place of the service of the Word through proclamation and sacraments."

Drama reminded Assembly participants that in Christ there can be no segregation of persons with disabilities from those who are "not yet disabled."

3. "How to respond as Lutherans to the role of the Holy Spirit in worship and how to provide for expression of particular spiritual gifts for the benefit of all (1 Cor. 12:7)."

4. How to make worship accessible to outsiders and thus a vehicle for mission, by keeping it "transparent and understandable."[6]

5. How to accomplish the necessary process of contextualizing worship while not imprisoning it in a certain socio-cultural setting and binding it to certain cultural norms.

6. How to "make better use of symbols, nonverbal elements, and architecture in the shaping of worship, and how to evaluate them theologically."

7. How to expand the participation of all the people of God in planning and leadership of worship services.

8. How to provide for exchange among member churches of worship "structures, texts, and above all hymns."

9. How to "remain in contact with ecumenical developments in worship and find ways to make them come alive in the life of the member churches."

10. How to create conditions "for the natural participation of children in worship so that its quality for all participants is enhanced."

Words to ponder

"Ulrich Bach has said that it would not misrepresent Paul to add to Galatians 3:28, 'There is neither handicapped nor non-handicapped for you are all one person in Christ.' "

> —Working Group paper on Participation of People with Disabling Conditions presented to LWF Seventh Assembly

"We have tended to form our communities of faith by gathering people of 'our kind.' In contrast, the clear direction of Jesus' ministry was one of incorporation, as he called the 'outsiders' of his day into a new community of acceptance and love. Paul also explicitly pictures the church as a community in which each diversity is invited to share its gifts to the whole (Gal. 3:28). . . . We call upon our churches to seek to develop a clearer missionary attention to the kingdom goal of incorporation by challenging each congregation to become more deliberately inclusive in its local outreach."

> —"Working Paper on Mission," received by the LWF Seventh Assembly (see note 2 above)

"Send us what we lack: persons skilled in personal evangelizing who are schooled in suffering, to work among us in our churches where the membership figures are hollow. In my country, at most 5% of our 5,000,000 nominal members are practicing Christians."

> —Morten Miland, youth delegate from the Evangelical Lutheran Church in Denmark, in appeal to the churches of the South, floor speech at Budapest Assembly

"While the opportunities for mission have become greater [in the South], many pastors from the South are moving up North for economic reasons . . . Even many of the good theologians in the South have been siphoned by the North . . . . Why don't the churches in the North employ workers from the churches of the South to serve . . . in other areas of the South? This way an affluent missionary life-style is not introduced in the poor areas of the South. And this is not only less expensive but will also be for the good of the churches in both South and North."

> —Dean José B. Fuliga of the Lutheran Theological Seminary in the Philippines, in a presentation on mission at the Seventh Assembly

"Modern media are neither entirely diabolic nor entirely benevolent; they have a potential for being both. They are instruments for illumination, recreation, reconciliation, and exploitation, depending on such complex factors as the orientation of their ownership, professional standards, and listener-viewer discrimination. In general, however, they are more likely to reinforce than to change, more likely to channel than to convert, more likely to entertain than to challenge."

> —*Signs of Hope* (Issue Material for the Working Groups, Seventh Assembly of the LWF), LWF Documentation 15/16 (March 1984): 85.

For discussion

1. Read the quotations at the beginning and end of the chapter, reflect on them, and share comments or questions about them.

2. What provisions are being made so that your church building, your worship, your education programs are fully accessible to persons with disabling conditions? Think of mobility, visual, and auditory impairment. What about mental or emotional disabilities? Discuss what the not-yet-disabled have to gain from the presence of persons with disabilities.

3. How does the group feel about the idea that a church's (congregation's) gifts are not given by God for its sole use or determination? If the poorer parts of the church have legitimate claim on the material resources of the richer parts, what can the rich ask from the poor?

4. Discuss the second quotation at the beginning of the chapter. Do members of the group agree that Lutherans have found it easier to be in ministry with poor people through social service, development, and advocacy activities than to incorporate them into the life and ministry

of the congregations? If so, what might be some reasons? How can we change?

5. Could the LWF guidelines for mission be part of your next annual meeting, or a mission Sunday emphasis? Could they influence a revision of your congregation's mission statement, if you have one? If you don't, could the guidelines stimulate the development of such a statement?

6. Should your congregation be more involved in communicating through such public media as radio and television? How can we prepare ourselves to deal with the new communication technologies as discriminating viewers and responsible citizens? What nonchurch communication can you point to which is telling the good news or being prophetic (announcing God's vision) today?

7. The worship report suggests that "contextualizing worship" is a good thing, while "imprisoning it in a certain socio-cultural setting" is bad. Can the group think of examples of each? Discuss where the group thinks each of the following would fit: singing black spirituals in a North American white congregation, in a North American black congregation; placing the nation's flag in the chancel area; avoiding the discussion of political questions in the sermon; accompanying the liturgy with pipe organ, with guitar, with jazz combo; praying for victorious performance by the athletes of one's country in the Olympics.

4

How Does the Family
Relate to Other Families?

"Christ is like a single body, which has many parts; it is still one body, even though it is made up of different parts. In the same way, all of us, whether Jews or Gentiles, whether slaves or free, have been baptized into the one body by the same Spirit, and we have all been given the one Spirit to drink."
—1 Corinthians 12:12-13 TEV

"We are on the way to unity. As the people of God called to fellowship in hope, we commit ourselves to God's fidelity. Even though we know that faith must reckon with experiences of darkness and with the reality of the cross, we also know that God will continue to do something 'new' with humanity and the world, and that the consummation of what we begin is his work alone and not a prolongation of our human possibilities."
—Cardinal Johannes Willebrands, president of the Vatican Secretariat for Promoting Christian Unity, in his address to the Budapest Assembly

The Lutheran family has always had a rather clear sense of its distinctiveness. It *means* something to be Lutheran—in terms of the confession of the Christian faith, with emphases such as those reviewed in Chapters 1 and 2 of this book.

Clergy from all parts of the Lutheran family served Communion together during Assembly services. Pictured are Pastor Elizabeth Lidell of Denmark and Pastor Tibor Hernád of Hungary.

Such a strong sense of identity has been a positive thing for the family. It helps family members to know who they are and where they stand on the basic elements of Christian faith. It also helps to build a feeling of unity and loyalty within the family.

But the same factors can also be negatives. They become that when they suggest to family members that they alone have a correct understanding of Christianity or that formal recognition of and work with the ministries of other Christians is not important. At times and for some Lutherans, such negatives have dominated the relationship with other families of the Christian faith.

The Lutheran churches working together through the Lutheran World Federation have sought in recent decades to build on the unity we seek with other Christian families, while remaining quite clear about that which continues to distinguish the various communities from each other. The differences, however, are more and more viewed as gifts, correctives, enrichments offered to each other, rather than causes of separation and competition. The Budapest Assembly took important new strides for Lutherans along the avenues of ecumenical understanding.

Ecumenical comes from a Greek word meaning "of the whole household of faith" and normally refers to the communities of believers *in Christ.* How such communities relate to Jewish believers is a matter for special attention. It is not part of the dialogues *within* Christianity and yet has a character different from all other interfaith contacts which Christians pursue. The Lutheran-Jewish relationship also took a large step forward because of what was done at Budapest and will be part of this chapter's discussion.

The unity we seek

For several decades, most of the major traditional families within Christianity have been trying to talk *with* each other—and to work with each other in addressing the world's needs. Whereas in previous centuries the emphasis was on talking at or about the other groups, stressing our differences—in the past 30 to 40 years the focus has shifted toward our unity, our commonality in faith and mission. This has been a worldwide development. The creation of the World Council of Churches in 1948 both expressed the yearning for more unity among Christians and has nurtured that yearning, in faith as well as mission or work together.

Globally, the families that have taken part in the quest for greater expression of Christian unity are: *Roman Catholics* (especially since Pope John XXIII and the Second Vatican Council of the early 1960s), *Eastern Orthodox, Anglicans* (known as Episcopalians in the U.S.), the *Reformed* churches (the theological tradition of Calvin, Zwingli, and Knox, including Presbyterians and Congregationalists), *Methodists, Baptists*—and *Lutherans.*

A strong ecumenical mandate is given to the LWF. Its constitution says the Federation shall "foster Lutheran interest in, concern for, and participation in the ecumenical movement." At its Sixth Assembly (Dar es Salaam, 1977) representatives of member churches endorsed the idea of unity in "reconciled diversity" as a concept providing "valuable help [for] the present phase" of the ecumenical task. The 1977 Assembly said it understood the concept of "reconciled diversity" as describing:

> a way to unity which does not automatically entail the surrender of confessional traditions and confessional identities. This way to unity is a way of living encounter, spiritual experience together, theological dialogue and mutual correction, a way in which the distinctiveness of each partner is not lost sight of, but is transformed and renewed, and in this way becomes visible and palpable to the other partners as a legitimate form of Christian existence and of

the one Christian faith. There is no glossing over the differences. Nor are the differences simply preserved and
maintained unaltered. On the contrary, they lose their di-
visive character and are reconciled to each other.[1]

The Budapest Assembly decided it was now time for
Lutherans to say something more about our understanding of Christian unity. It adopted a brief statement, presented as flowing from previous statements of both the
LWF and the World Council of Churches (such as those
of WCC assemblies in 1961 and 1975). The Budapest language avoids using either "reconciled diversity" (LWF
1977) or "conciliar fellowship" (WCC 1975). Instead, the
1984 LWF statement speaks of the one church in Christ
as "a communion within which diversities contribute to
its fullness . . . , a committed fellowship, able to make
common decisions and to act in common." The full text
follows:

The Unity We Seek

The true unity of the church, which is the unity of the
body of Christ and participates in the unity of the Father,
Son and Holy Spirit, is given in and through proclamation
of the gospel in Word and sacrament. This unity is expressed
as a communion in the common and, at the same time,
multiform confession of one and the same apostolic faith.
It is a communion in holy baptism and in the eucharistic
meal, a communion in which the ministries exercised are
recognized by all as expressions of the ministry instituted
by Christ in his church. It is a communion where diversities
contribute to fullness and are no longer barriers to unity.
It is a committed fellowship, able to make common decisions and to act in common.

The diversity present in this communion rises out of the
differing cultural and ethnic contexts in which the one
church of Christ lives out its mission and the number of
church traditions in which the apostolic faith has been

maintained, transmitted and lived throughout the centuries. In recognizing these diversities as expressions of the one apostolic faith and the one catholic church, traditions are changed, antagonisms overcome, and mutual condemnations lifted. The diversities are reconciled and transformed into a legitimate and indispensable multiformity within the one Body of Christ.

This communion lives out its unity in confessing the one apostolic faith. It assembles in worship and in intercession for all people. It is active in common witness to Jesus Christ; in advocacy for the weak, poor, and oppressed; and in striving for peace, justice, and freedom. It is ordered in all its components in conciliar structures and actions. It is in need of constant renewal and is, at the same time, a foretaste of that communion which the Lord will at the end of time bring about in his kingdom.

A single family within the universal church, such as the Lutheran family, finds itself exploring unity with other families in two formal settings. One is that of full ecumenical conversation, which is *multilateral,* including as many parties as wish to participate. The other is that of the *bilateral* conversation, where Lutherans engage one other tradition at a time. We Lutherans are committed to a half dozen such bilateral, interconfessional dialogues. In addition to the international conversations, both multilateral and bilateral, some member churches of the LWF are engaged in similar conversations at a national level. That is true of Lutheran churches in Canada and the United States.

It requires a fairly fat catalog or scorecard just to keep tabs on all these conversations.[2] The key facts about them are (1) that they are happening at all, (2) that they are resulting in genuine progress toward greater understanding among the churches of their unity amid diversity, (3) that they represent the churches at the level of national/ international structures and reflect the thinking of the churches' theological leaders. This last point intends to say that, while the churches' conversations about unity have a certain official status, for the most part the results thus far have had little practical impact on the thinking and behavior of Christians in local churches and communities. We will return to this issue later in this chapter.

Baptism, eucharist, ministry

As the most exciting and far-reaching current example of multilateral conversation in which many Christian traditions are jointly engaged, let us look at the quest for a new expression of unity represented by "Baptism, Eucharist and Ministry" (BEM). This document, produced through a process coordinated by the World Council of Churches and adopted at the Lima (Peru) meeting of its Faith and Order Commission (1982), is now referred to the churches worldwide for study and response.[3]

In assessing the document, a working group on BEM at the Budapest Assembly said: "This is not simply another theological conversation among Christians, but a new stage. Something is happening. An attempt is being made to transcend traditional disputes." The working group also asked Lutherans not to see more in the document than is there:

> We are aware that BEM is not an attempt to produce a new ecumenical creed or to lead to a super-church. BEM has achieved convergence, not consensus. We regard BEM as an important step toward unity in reconciled diversity, that is, by means of a mutual recognition of baptism, eucharist, and ministry to reach a new dimension of unity with other Christians.[4]

The BEM working group at Budapest expressed both gratitude and concern about each of the three sections of the document:

1. Baptism

Gratitude for emphases on baptism's connection with the communion of saints, the ethical consequences of baptism, and eschatological dimension of baptism.

Concern that putting infant baptism and believer's baptism on a par makes it seem that it does not matter which is used. Baptism as "solely God's saving act" is not sufficiently stressed.

2. Eucharist

Gratitude for focus on thanksgiving and joy, the Holy Spirit and the Trinity, and the Eucharist's relationship to the whole of life.

Concern that Lutherans should celebrate the Eucharist with more frequency (weekly is recommended) and that Lutherans should give more attention to the theological idea of *epiklesis* (invocation of the Holy Spirit at the close of the Eucharistic Prayer).

3. Ministry

Gratitude that BEM spotlights the variety of forms of ministry found in the New Testament and challenges Lutherans to ask if they should use its threefold pattern of ministry (deacon, presbyter, bishop) and adopt the sign of apostolic succession for bishops as an additional gift which would help in our quest for unity with many other traditions.

Concern that BEM's description of the interplay between clergy and laity does not permit "the laity to have a leading role in the sense customarily practiced in the Lutheran tradition."

The Assembly in Budapest received the report containing these expressions of gratitude and concern, and then adopted two recommendations:

1. That the LWF member churches be urged (*a*) to study BEM, if possible with other churches participating in the

WCC Faith and Order Commission; (*b*) to use BEM and the Lima Liturgy (a worship order lifting up BEM's concerns) "as a stimulus to church renewal and as an instrument for examining our Lutheran tradition"; (*c*) to share the results of BEM study with both the WCC and the LWF; (*d*) to use "Growth in Ecumenical Commitment" as a resource for the study of BEM.[5]

2. That the LWF Studies Department (and its Strasbourg Institute for Ecumenical Research) "support the member churches in their study of the BEM texts through consultative services."

The bilateral dialogues

The world Lutheran family has on its platter at present theological conversations with six other Christian communions. A summary of the status of each, with pertinent recommendations adopted at Budapest, follows:

1. *Roman Catholic.* This dialogue, launched in 1967, was the first entered by the Vatican after the close of the Second Vatican Council. It has had an equally high priority for Lutherans. It is now entering a new phase, in which special attention will be given to the understandings of the papacy and the place of Mary, mother of our Lord. No action was taken by the Assembly, but a working group report suggested that member churches consider steps that can be taken to express the growth in fellowship with Roman Catholics, such as expansion of the invitation to each other's eucharistic altars, which would be especially helpful "for those who live in mixed marriages." The report also expressed this concern about the papacy:

> . . . in our churches and congregations as well as in theology, the papacy, as it has developed historically and has been doctrinally defined within the Roman Catholic Church at the First Vatican Council [1870], appears as a particularly serious problem in respect to the community

of our churches. For the Lutheran church . . . the hope for full community includes the hope for a papacy under the gospel within the framework of the renewal of all our churches. . . .

2. *Orthodox*. This dialogue was begun on the international level in 1981. Its comprehensive goal is "total fellowship as full mutual recognition." The report received at Budapest said, "This dialogue will not quickly yield results in the form of agreed doctrinal statements." The Assembly adopted one recommendation:

• to ask the member churches to study using a liturgical version of the Nicene Creed in which we would say "We believe in the Holy Spirit . . . who proceeds from the Father" rather than ". . . from the Father and the Son." (The latter formulation is one Lutherans inherited as part of the Western church, which added it to the original language shared earlier by both Eastern and Western Christians. Inclusion of "and the Son" continues to be a stumbling block to the Orthodox, who confess that the Spirit proceeds from the Father only.)

3. *Anglican*. International conversations were held 1970-1972. Out of these and regional Anglican/Lutheran dialogues have come suggested steps toward full church fellowship. The U.S. Lutheran/Episcopal dialogue led to the September 1982 decisions by the Episcopal Church and the three U.S. LWF member churches to enter "interim eucharistic sharing." The result is that many U.S. Lutherans and Episcopalians are now able to receive the Lord's Supper at each others' altars. The Assembly voted:

• to urge other member churches to consider negotiating similar agreements with neighboring Anglican churches, and to ask appropriate LWF departments to consider the feasibility of undertaking certain study and work projects jointly with the Anglican communion.

4. *Reformed*. A new dialogue is beginning in 1985, with the World Alliance of Reformed Churches organizing the Reformed participation. A regional agreement in Europe has led to church fellowship among Lutheran, Reformed, and Union (combination of Lutheran and Reformed) churches. Called the Leuenberg Agreement, it has also been adopted, in part, in Latin America. The Assembly agreed:

• to ask appropriate LWF departments to consider the feasibility of undertaking certain study and work projects jointly with the World Alliance of Reformed Churches.

5. *Methodist*. Lutherans have not had many obvious doctrinal differences with Methodists; those differences which exist are more in piety, spirituality, Christian behavior, and the character of worship and congregational life. International dialogue has gone on since 1979 and there is hope that recommendations on first steps toward church fellowship will be forthcoming in future years. The Assembly voted:

• if the possibility arises in the future, appropriate LWF departments should consider the feasibility of undertaking study and work projects jointly with the World Methodist Council.

6. *Baptist*. A joint commission of the LWF and the Baptist World Alliance is beginning dialogue in 1985.

The Jewish connection is unique

There has always been something special about the relationship between Jews and Lutherans. The two families of faith both have roots in the Hebrew Scriptures. Study of the Old Testament was a key part of the theological work of Martin Luther. While their interpretations of the Hebrew Bible have important variations, there is much on which Lutherans and Jews can agree.

But in a negative way, also, the Jewish-Lutheran relationship has been special. Clouding it ever since the time of the Reformation, and with particular horror the past five decades, has been material written by Luther which is violent and virulently anti-Jewish. Luther's writings against the Jews, couched in religious language and expressing his deep disappointment that in the wake of the Reformation most did not convert to belief in Christ, have been used to support racial and political anti-Semitism around the world, notably in Europe during the past 100 years. The Hitler period, culminating in the Holocaust—the greatest tragedy ever to befall the Jewish people—drew upon Luther's anti-Jewish writings, and many observers see those writings as one important element in creating a climate of acceptance for the Nazi program of Jewish annihilation.

Lutheran-Jewish conversations have been under way in Europe and North America for more than 30 years, stimulated in large part by the experience of the Nazi years and the Holocaust. In recent years, two formal conversations between Jewish and Lutheran theologians, sponsored by the International Jewish Committee for Interreligious Consultation and the Lutheran World Federation, have been held. The second of these, during the 500th anniversary year of Luther's birth (July 1983, Stockholm), deliberately focused on "Luther, Lutheranism, and the Jews." Its report has three parts: statements by Lutheran participants, by Jewish participants, and jointly by both. The Lutheran portion of the statement contains explicit and unqualified disavowal of Luther's anti-Jewish writings:

> We hold that an honest, historical treatment of Luther's attacks on the Jews takes away from modern anti-Semites the assumption that they may legitimately call on the authority of Luther's name to bless their anti-Semitism. We

insist that Luther does not support racial anti-Semitism, nationalistic anti-Semitism, or political anti-Semitism. Even the deplorable religious anti-Semitism of the 16th century, to which Luther's attacks made important contributions, is a horrible anachronism when translated to the conditions of the modern world. We recognize with deep regret, however, that Luther has been used to justify such anti-Semitism in the period of national socialism and that his writings lent themselves to such abuse.

Witness—yes; proselytizing—no

The joint portion of the statement included these paragraphs:

Meeting in Stockholm, we are mindful of the compassionate response of Scandinavian Christians to the plight of Jewish victims of Nazi persecution forty years ago. This spirit renews our faith in the human capacity to confront evil with courage and determination.

The deliberations on the theme of "Luther, Lutheranism, and the Jews" were informed by an openness of views and a spirit of mutual respect for the integrity and dignity of our faith communities. The discussions revealed a depth of mutual understanding and trust.

1. We affirm the integrity and dignity of our two faith communities and repudiate any organized proselytizing of each other.

2. We pledge to combat all forms of racial and religious prejudice and express our solidarity with all who suffer the denial of full religious freedom.

3. Sharing in the common patrimony of the prophets of Israel and inspired by their vision, we commit ourselves to strive for a world in which the threat of nuclear warfare will be ended, where poverty and hunger will be eradicated, in which violence and terrorism will be overcome, and a just and lasting peace will be established.

Hungarian Lutheran hospitality included food and fellowship in more than 100 parishes during the Assembly.

In a footnote on "Organized Proselytizing," the report of the Stockholm meeting uses the following definition of proselytizing, and indicates that a Jewish participant found it "altogether acceptable" in clarifying "the distinction between mission or witness and proselytism."

> Proselytism embraces whatever violates the right of the human person, Christian or non-Christian, to be free from external coercion in religious matters, or whatever, in the proclamation of the Gospel, does not conform to the ways God draws free men to himself in response to his calls to serve in spirit and in truth.[6]

The Stockholm statement's footnote on proselytism adds that the Jewish participant, in response to a question, said, "Many of us in the Jewish delegation feel the need to specify the word 'organized' in this case. The activity of organized groups that set out consciously to undermine the faith commitment of Jews is offensive to us."

The Budapest Assembly voted to "receive with gratitude the statements" on "Luther, Lutheranism, and the Jews" and commend them to the member churches for their study and consideration in their relationships with the Jewish people.[7] The Assembly also voted (1) to ask the LWF to continue its work in the area of Jewish-Christian relations; (2) to urge continued consultations with "our Jewish partners"; and (3) to encourage the member churches to support the work of Jewish-Christian dialogue.

Budapest was the first LWF Assembly at which a speaker from outside the Christian family was given the platform. He was Dr. Gerhard M. Riegner, recently retired as general secretary of the World Jewish Congress. In his address he expressed gratitude for the Stockholm statement and for the special attention the LWF has given to Jewish-Lutheran relations. He referred to the fact that LWF's staff desk on the Church and the Jewish People is not part of its unit on "other faiths and ideologies" (which deals with such concerns as Islam, Buddhism, and Marxism). Then Dr. Riegner offered this comment on the special nature of the relationships between Jews and all of the Christian family:

[Our] mutual relationship . . . is indeed a very special one. It differs considerably from those you have with other faith communities. . . . I do not think that this relationship is ambiguous. It is determined on the one hand by the fact that, not being Christians, we do not belong to the Christian *oekumene* [the ecumenical household]. It is determined, on the other hand, by the fact that special links exist between our two traditions, which do not exist between the Christian churches and any other living faith community.

Words to ponder

"We need to be troubled at times . . . about our stance within the family of Christian churches. While never denying the contribution that is the burden of the Reformation, as the Lutheran contribution, it is necessary to remember that the Lutheran Church is also in constant need of reform. We have much to receive from the ecumenical movement. We cannot be the same if we enter into this movement of all Christians, seeking the unity of the church, in order that the world may believe."

> —Carl H. Mau Jr., in report of the Lutheran World Federation general secretary to the Budapest Assembly

"Without minimizing our apostolic faith, can we not now maximize our apostolic order [by accepting the historic succession of bishops]? As current Roman Catholics are purifying their obedience to the fullness of the apostolic faith, are we Lutherans, as evangelical catholics, able to recover our catholic participation in the fullness of apostolic order? Without such doctrinally-permissible mutual accommodations, it is highly unlikely that there will be any major ecumenical advance in our time. . . ."

> —William H. Lazareth of the United States, in his presentation on ecumenics to the Budapest Assembly

"Does it make any difference for our lands and our societies that there are churches in their midst? The answer to that question is decisive and sometimes the inability to make the unity we confess in every Sunday worship visible in our daily life amidst our societies is, like salt, losing its savor. Being in a minority is not itself a problem—salt is always less than that which should be salted. The problem is whether the fragmented pieces of salt together can salt."

—Soritura Nababan of Indonesia, in a response to William Lazareth's presentation at the Budapest Assembly

"We know that witness is an essential trait of the Christian community. Our condemnation of proselytism . . . deals with immoral and indecent methods of persuading others to change their faith. . . . While we do not question the right of anybody to witness, and while we have ourselves our own eschatological expectations, we believe that there should not be institutions which are especially directed at the Jewish community."

—Gerhard M. Riegner, retired general secretary of the World Jewish Congress, in his address to the Budapest Assembly

"I pray that they may all be one . . . so that the world will believe that you sent me."

—Jesus in prayer to the Father,
John 17:21 (TEV)

For discussion

1. Read the quotations at chapter's beginning and end, reflect on them, and share comments or questions about them.

2. Make a list of the elements you believe fit under the category of "Lutheran distinctiveness." Talk about the positives and the negatives associated with the items listed.

3. How do group members view the Budapest Assembly's statement on "The Unity We Seek"? Are you experiencing as a fact, in your own locale, that antagonisms are being reconciled and condemnations lifted? Do you

see changes in the relationships among faith traditions to be a sign of hope?

4. Has your congregation had opportunity to discuss the results of ecumenical dialogue—either such multilateral documents as "Baptism, Eucharist and Ministry" or the bilateral Episcopal/Lutheran or Roman Catholic/Lutheran agreements? If not, how might such discussions be organized in your congregation?

5. How does the group feel about the distinction between witnessing to Jewish people as one would witness to any people and maintaining organized missions to the Jews?

6. Make a list of things your congregation has done in the past year to bring about greater unity within God's total household of faith. What is it that builds unity among believers, yet allows diversity?

5

How Does the Family Maintain Its Unity?

"If your brother sins against you, go to him and show him his fault. . . . If he listens to you, you have won your brother back. But if he will not listen to you, take one or two other persons with you. . . . And if he will not listen to them, then tell the whole thing to the church."
—Matthew 18:15-17a TEV

"The great disgrace of these four centuries is that Lutheran churches have become captive to territory and nation. There is no united Lutheran witness to the Gospel world-wide. It is my hope that God will in the next century free us from such captivity."

—official visitor from the Evangelical Lutheran Church of Brazil, in discussion on global Lutheran witness at Budapest Assembly

A large, worldwide family of faith, as we have seen, gives careful thought to its relationships with other faith communities. It must also pay attention to its own internal unity. What does it mean for churches to be part of the global Lutheran family? The Budapest Assembly of the Lutheran World Federation dealt with three aspects of the family unity question:

1. How do the churches understand their work together through the Lutheran World Federation? (LWF's identity and task)
2. How do the churches view their relationship with the other churches which hold LWF membership? (Defining interchurch fellowship)
3. How do the member churches hold each other to account within the LWF community? (Suspension of membership over the apartheid question)

The quest for global Lutheran unity

Lutherans around the world have never had a single, unified, international church body. Most denominational families don't. The Roman Catholics are the obvious exception. They do have a single global structure, led by one person (the pope), with a central decision making authority (the Vatican in Rome).

Most Lutheran church bodies developed as entities co-terminous with either nations (Church of Norway, Evangelical Lutheran Church of Canada) or regions within what have become nations (Evangelical Lutheran Church of Saxony, Slovak Evangelical Lutheran Church of the Augsburg Confession). Each of these Lutheran churches is autonomous—that is, accountable to no higher human authority than itself.

How, then, can these many Lutheran churches of the one planet Earth express the unity they believe they have? *Not* by forming themselves into a single, international "Lutheran Church of the World." *Not* by electing a single authoritative leader, a Lutheran pope. Neither of these possibilities has ever received serious consideration.

But some visible expression of unity within the world family of Lutherans has been a hope since early in this century, if not before. This desire gave rise to the formation of the Lutheran World Convention in 1923, and then to its successor, the Lutheran World Federation, in 1947. The

Federation has been seen by its member churches as their vehicle for making a united Lutheran witness to the faith, for conducting joint mission and service, and for coordinating the family's relationships with other families of faith.

What member churches expect to do together through the LWF is formally expressed in the Federation constitution, in a statement of six functions. As amended by the Budapest Assembly, they read:

... the Lutheran World Federation shall:

1. Further a united witness before the world to the gospel of Jesus Christ as the power of God for salvation.
2. Cultivate unity of faith and confession among the Lutheran churches of the world.
3. Develop community and cooperation in study among Lutherans.
4. Foster Lutheran interest in, concern for, and participation in the ecumenical movement.
5. Support Lutheran churches and groups as they endeavor to extend the gospel and carry out the mission given to the church.
6. Help Lutheran churches and groups, as a sharing community, to serve human need and to promote social and economic justice and human rights.[1]

LWF's self-understanding and task

During the years leading up to the 1984 Assembly, much reflecting on the identity and role of the LWF took place within its member churches. Among the possible understandings of the Federation, these three have emerged with serious support:

1. LWF as an organization of member churches, a federation with no power over its members except that which they choose to give it.
2. LWF as a world confessional family within the larger family of Christian communities.

Voting on key issues at the Assembly was by secret ballot.

3. LWF as a form or expression of the Lutheran church at a global level, reflected in pulpit and altar fellowship among its member churches.

The three understandings are not mutually exclusive, of course. Some people have argued for one or another over the rest. But others have attempted to retain elements of all three emphases.

The Budapest Assembly took two actions related to the matter of LWF's self-understanding and task. Together, they undoubtedly represent one of the more significant outcomes of the 1984 family gathering of Lutherans, because of the new clarity they give to the meaning of the global Lutheran community and the Lutheran World Federation as one of its instruments.

First, the Assembly voted to transmit to the member churches for their attention and study two reports which summarize the discussions within the member churches of the Federation's identity and task:[2]

- *Self-Understanding and Ecumenical Role of the Lutheran World Federation* (Geneva: LWF Studies, 1984)
- *Growth in Ecumenical Commitment* (Geneva: LWF Studies, 1984)

Second, Budapest adopted as a public statement a six-paragraph expression of the member churches' current understanding of their relationship to (1) the church universal, (2) the global Lutheran community, (3) each other within the LWF, and (4) the LWF as an instrument of their global identity and mission. The statement follows:

Statement on the Self-Understanding and Task of the LWF

As Lutheran churches we confess and affirm the unity of the one universal church, which is the body of Christ in this world. We know ourselves to be called to give witness to that unity through faith and love, together with other Christians in all continents.

We give witness to and affirm the communion in which the Lutheran churches of the world are bound together. This communion is rooted in the unity of the apostolic faith as given in the Holy Scriptures and witnessed by the ecumenical creeds and the Lutheran confessions. It is based on "united witness before the world to the gospel of Jesus Christ as the power of God for salvation" (Constitution of the LWF, III.2.a). And it is based on agreement in the proclamation of the gospel and celebration of the sacraments (Augsburg Confession VII).

This Lutheran communion of churches finds its visible expression in pulpit and altar fellowship, in common witness and service, in the joint fulfillment of the missionary task, and in openness to ecumenical cooperation, dialogue, and community. The Lutheran churches of the world consider their communion as an expression of the one, holy, catholic, and apostolic church. Thus they are committed to work for the manifestation of the unity of the church given in Jesus Christ.

The LWF is an expression and instrument of this communion. It assists it to become more and more a conciliar, mutually committed communion by furthering consultation and exchange among its member churches and other churches of the Lutheran tradition, as well as by furthering mutual participation in each other's joys, sufferings, and struggles. Through the LWF its member churches are enabled and supported to witness together to the gospel, to serve jointly in this world, and to act ecumenically with one accord. At the same time, the LWF also strengthens the one ecumenical movement of which it considers itself to be a part and to which it contributes through its own ecumenical efforts, as well as through relationships and cooperation with other Christian world communions and the World Council of Churches.

The kind of authority the LWF possesses is a delegated authority entrusted to the Federation by its member churches for particular purposes. It is also a moral authority which is lodged in the inner persuasive power of decisions that are submitted to the member churches for their reception.

The communion of Lutheran churches served and expressed by the LWF is open to others. The LWF invites, therefore, all churches that are committed to the Lutheran confessions or see themselves in agreement with its doctrinal basis to become members of the communion of the LWF or enter into closer relationship with it.

All members in full fellowship

Another major step taken by the Budapest Assembly toward clarifying the unity question was adoption of a constitutional amendment on mutual recognition among the member churches. The amendment says simply: "The member churches of the Lutheran World Federation understand themselves to be in pulpit and altar fellowship with each other."

"Pulpit and altar fellowship" is the term traditionally used by Lutherans for what other Christians call "full communion." It means that, for the churches declaring such fellowship, their pulpits are open to each other's pastors and their altars are open to each other's communicants. The effect is to recognize fully the ministries of each other's churches.

Many of the member churches of the LWF have so recognized other member churches in the past, but it has not been universal among the Federation's churches. The practical consequence of the action is that any church joining the Federation henceforth—and each of the present members—declares that in accepting the LWF's doctrinal basis it is also willing to accept fully the ministries of all other churches which do so. The LWF doctrinal basis reads:

> The Lutheran World Federation acknowledges the Holy Scriptures of the Old and New Testaments as the only source and the infallible norm of all church doctrine and practice, and sees in the three Ecumenical Creeds and in the Confessions of the Lutheran Church, especially in the Unaltered Augsburg Confession and Luther's Small Catechism, a pure exposition of the Word of God.

The vote on accepting the constitutional amendment concerning fellowship was one-sided but not unanimous (261 for, 27 against, 9 abstaining). Delegates from the Lutheran Church in Korea and the India Evangelical Lutheran Church were among those who spoke against the amendment. They and four other LWF member churches are partner churches of the Lutheran Church–Missouri

Synod of the United States, which is not an LWF member. The Missouri Synod does not consider itself in communion with most other Lutheran churches, for it requires full doctrinal agreement as a prerequisite. It differs from some other Lutheran churches on such issues as ordination of women and biblical interpretation.

There is general agreement that the Budapest actions on Lutheran unity and the LWF's identity have produced a more churchlike authority for the Federation. The member churches have said they want the LWF to serve as a global expression of Lutheranism in a deeper sense than it has previously. They have also agreed to recognize each other in a more complete way than had been the case, based on mutual membership in the Federation.

Can a member be suspended?

The membership question was posed in yet another way for the "family" meeting in Budapest: When does a member church forfeit the privileges of membership?

The issue came to the Assembly because of the refusal of two German-speaking member churches in southern Africa to (1) denounce publicly and unequivocally the apartheid system as incompatible with the Christian faith, and (2) move toward unity with the predominantly black churches in the region. The white churches are the 12,000-member German Evangelical Lutheran Church in South-West Africa (Namibia) and the 6000-member Evangelical Lutheran Church in Southern Africa (Cape Church).

It was the third Assembly in a row at which the question of apartheid and the relationship of member churches to it and to each other became an agenda item. A review of the 14 years of history will be useful.

1970—Evian. At this Assembly the LWF voted to endorse the principles that (1) in the Lutheran church, members of all races should be willing at all times to receive communion together, and (2) Lutheran churches should oppose the principles and practices of racial discrimination and segregation. The Evian Assembly also recommended to the LWF Executive Committee that:

1. A delegation be sent from the LWF to churches where the above principles constitute a special problem to urge them to bring their racial practices into conformity with the principles of Christian fellowship as rapidly as possible. . . .
2. In order to encourage the quest for equal justice the two principles shall serve as criteria in providing assistance to churches.

A meeting of southern African Lutheran leaders was held to deal with the issue, at Hammanskraal, South Africa, in 1971, and an LWF delegation headed by Dr. Mikko Juva, then president of the LWF, visited the churches involved in 1972. The executive committee and the program arms of the LWF made numerous efforts to assist the southern African churches to move to a common witness and structure. In 1975 at Swakopmund, Namibia, an appeal was made to the churches of the Federation of Evangelical Lutheran Churches in Southern Africa (which includes both white and black churches), emphasizing the importance of organic union in view of the apartheid situation in their societies. The Swakopmund Appeal included these words:

We affirm that the political system in force in South Africa, with its discrimination against some sectors of the population, its acceptance of the break-up of many families, its concentration of power in the hands of one race only, and the limitations it imposes on freedom, cannot be reconciled with the gospel of the grace of God in Jesus Christ. We affirm that this system in many ways hinders the exercise of Christian fellowship.

In 1975, four regional Lutheran churches in South Africa of mostly black membership united to form the Evangelical Lutheran Church of Southern Africa (ELCSA). White Lutherans in South Africa had been involved early in the process of negotiating the formation of the new church, but decided against joining it.

1977—Dar es Salaam. Here the LWF adopted a resolution called "Southern Africa: Confessional Integrity." It included these words:

> Confessional subscription is more than a formal acknowledgment of doctrine. Churches which have signed the confessions of the church thereby commit themselves to show through their daily witness and service that the gospel has empowered them to live as the people of God. They also commit themselves to accept in their worship and at the table of the Lord the brothers and sisters who belong to other churches that accept the same confessions. Confessional subscription should lead to concrete manifestations in unity in worship and in working together at the common tasks of the church.
>
> Under normal circumstances Christians may have different opinions in political questions. However, political and social systems may become so perverted and oppressive that it is consistent with the confession to reject them and to work for changes. We especially appeal to our white member churches in southern Africa to recognize that the situation in southern Africa constitutes a *status confessionis*. That means that, on the basis of faith and in order to manifest the unity of the church, churches would publicly and unequivocally reject the existing apartheid system.

After the Dar es Salaam Assembly there was hope that the white churches in southern Africa might respond to the clear call for unity with the black churches and for expression of solidarity with them in public rejection of the apartheid system. But there was no movement of any substance. Meanwhile, the socio-political situation in both South Africa and Namibia worsened for the black population.

In December 1983, at the pre-Budapest Assembly consultation for delegates from Africa, held at Harare, Zimbabwe, recommendations to the Budapest Assembly were adopted asking that:

- the Assembly reaffirm the Dar es Salaam statement on "Status Confessionis" and call upon the "white" member churches to take positive steps toward church unity;
- as an interim measure the "white" member churches be suspended from the LWF membership until such time as they reject apartheid publicly and unequivocally and move toward unity with other member churches in the area.

Budapest votes to suspend

So the issue came for decision to Budapest in 1984. There was discussion throughout the Assembly, including references to the question in many speeches from platform and floor, and one full evening was given to an open hearing on the subject. Representatives of the white churches in southern Africa said progress was being made, suspension would worsen relations between white and black Lutherans in the region, and more time was needed to achieve the goals stated by the 1970 and 1977 assemblies. Black church representatives replied that no meaningful progress had occurred, that the white Lutherans had not accepted black offers of fellowship at the congregational level, that the whites showed no willingness to join the blacks in suffering because of the apartheid system, and that after 14 years of waiting the only move proving the Federation to be serious about its previous statements would be suspension of membership.

Church leaders from southern Africa held a press conference during the Seventh Assembly. Pictured are (from left): Pastor Zephaniah Kameeta of Namibia, Pastor Wilfred J. Blank of Namibia, Pastor Christoph Brandt of South Africa, Bishop Manas Buthelezi of South Africa, Pastor T. Simon Farisani of South Africa.

Delegates from other parts of the world joined the discussion. Some of the representatives of churches in Germany (both the Federal Republic and the Democratic Republic) which continue to send personnel and financial support to the southern Africa German-speaking churches also asked for more time and postponement of suspension. Virtually all of the other voices from outside southern Africa, however, supported suspension.

In a surprise move, the night of the open hearing on suspension, the two white churches, via letters with identical wording, announced to the Assembly that they were voluntarily suspending themselves or, as the German of their letters was translated, going on "dormant membership." They were joined by a third German-speaking church, the 15,000-member Evangelical Lutheran Church in Southern Africa (Natal-Transvaal), which had been an applicant for membership in the Federation as the Assembly opened but was now withdrawing its application.

When at last the Assembly voted on the suspension resolution, by secret ballot and following a time of prayer, the result was: 222 in favor (81%), 23 opposed (8%), 29 abstaining (11%). The two-thirds majority required for passage was met. The text of the resolution is:

The Seventh Assembly, having studied and heard extensive reports regarding the situation in southern Africa:

1. REAFFIRMS the resolution of the Sixth Assembly (Dar es Salaam, 1977) on "Southern Africa: Confessional Integrity."

2. Strongly and urgently APPEALS to its white member churches in southern Africa, namely the Evangelical Lutheran Church in Southern Africa (Cape Church) and the German Evangelical Lutheran Church in South-West Africa (Namibia) to publicly and unequivocally reject the system of apartheid (separate development) and to end the division of the church on racial grounds.

3. Regretfully concluding that no satisfactory fulfillment of this goal has as yet been achieved, FINDS that those churches have in fact withdrawn from the confessional community which forms the basis of membership in the Lutheran World Federation. Therefore, the Assembly is constrained to SUSPEND the membership of the above churches, intending that such action serve as a help for those churches to come to clear witness against the policy of apartheid (separate development) and to move to visible unity of the Lutheran churches in southern Africa.

4. UNDERSTANDS that suspension means that those churches are not entitled to send voting delegates to an

LWF Assembly or official meeting, nor to have any of their members on a governing organ of the Federation.

5. INSTRUCTS the Executive Committee to lift this suspension if satisfactory actions are taken by the churches involved to establish the legal and practical conditions for abolishing the practice of apartheid in the life of the churches and their congregations.

6. OFFERS the Lutheran churches in southern Africa every support and assistance as they seek to witness to the Gospel of the grace of Jesus Christ and move to visible unity. Such support and assistance should include the following:

   a. A visit of a delegation of the Federation to counsel with and encourage the Lutheran churches of southern Africa.

   b. Encouraging other regular visits to the churches by member churches and the Federation.

   c. Continued appeal to member churches around the world to support all Lutheran churches and all churches in southern Africa by prayer.

   d. Continued commitment to strong advocacy on the part of the LWF and its member churches seeking to support peaceful and positive change towards equality of all peoples in the societies of southern Africa.

7. ENCOURAGES all member churches to engage in ongoing self-examination in the light of Scripture, rejecting all forms of racial discrimination.

We, like our societies, are infected with racism, and therefore the LWF and each of our churches carries the disease of racism. We confess the sin of racism. We repent for the harm it continues to inflict on the lives of people. We commit ourselves to change. We call on our churches to examine their lives, to repent of their sins of racism, and to take action to reform their lives.

Still in the family?

Suspension was interpreted as different from expulsion. The two churches continue to be listed on the LWF roster of member churches, but with certain privileges removed for what it is hoped will be a temporary period. To use the family analogy, it is as though a wayward son or daughter has been put on probation until showing that he or she will repent and live by the family's understanding of what membership in that family means. The wayward one is not ousted from the family and may continue to attend family gatherings, but without the privilege of participation in family decisions.

It is not clear if the action will move the white and black churches in South Africa and Namibia toward unity, in either the short or long term. What is clear is that the Lutheran world family as a whole wishes to state clearly that the apartheid system is a violation of the will of God and thus cannot be a matter of indifference to the people of God. A summary of the theological reasons for that position has been offered by Dr. Robert Bertram, a theologian of the Association of Evangelical Lutheran Churches in the United States:[3]

1. Making racial identity an essential for fellowship in the church is not permissible. Adding *anything* to the gospel in fact diminishes the gospel (see Paul's word to the Galatians on circumcision).

2. Acceptance of apartheid in the church allows secular authority to displace the authority in the church of the gospel and the sacraments.

3. Apartheid's character is antiecumenical, splintering Christ's body within the same confessing community.

Budapest took these additional actions related to the suspension issue:

1. Asked member churches that provide financial and personnel support to the suspended churches, in consultation with the other Lutheran churches in the region, to reconsider that support and either suspend it or assure that it assists the white churches toward reconciliation with their black sisters and brothers. If there is no positive

movement by the suspended churches by January 1987, the supporting churches are asked to terminate all financial and personnel support at that time.

2. Urged the other member churches in South Africa and Namibia to pray for the suspended churches, continue to welcome them into fellowship, and offer them financial and personnel resources.

3. Urged all member churches to express opposition to apartheid by "visible and concrete steps, including boycott of goods and withdrawal of investments, to end all economic and cultural support of apartheid, even as they continue to urge their own governments, business organizations, and trade unions to observe strict enforcement of military and oil embargoes and boycotts concerning culture, sports, the transfer of nuclear technology, and the importation of nuclear materials. . . ."

4. Asked each member church to combat all forms of racism in its own life and that of its nation, and to report to the LWF executive committee by January 1988 on steps taken to eradicate institutional racism from its structures, for the purpose of sharing with other member churches.

The entire experience was, like any attempt at constructive discipline within a family, a mixture of pain and joy. There was pain that members of the family should need to be publicly called to account, and joy that the global family of LWF member churches could, in the end, after 14 years, take actions that were, as one delegate put it, "more than just more words."

Words to ponder

"There are Lutherans who continue to question the confessional integrity of other Lutherans. It is difficult for them to become members of the Federation, because they believe this would bring them into "fellowship" with Lutherans with whom they are not in sufficient doctrinal agreement. We are troubled, however, by what we perceive to be a legalistic use of Confessions of the Lutheran movement. We are troubled by the fact that these churches are moving toward greater isolation from the rest of the Lutheran community. We must. . .try to reverse that trend, for they are a part of the Lutheran communion."

> —Carl H. Mau Jr., in report of the LWF general secretary to the Budapest Assembly

"The desire is strong in my church for identification with a world family of Lutherans. If LWF affiliation does not mean that, we would have a problem."

> —delegate from the Evangelical Church of the Augsburg Confession in Romania, during discussion at Budapest Assembly

"So close is [our] bond that it is no accident that . . . both the Lutheran and Reformed churches have found it necessary to speak of a *status* or *casus confessionis*. I refer to the question of the theological or moral justification of the apartheid system. . . . The declaration of *status confessionis*, it seems to me, furnishes the Lutheran World Federation and the World Alliance of Reformed Churches with common ground of a new kind. Henceforward, the dialogue between our two families cannot possibly bypass this question. . . . The point will be to achieve still greater clarity as to the consequences which flow from this declaration for the witness of the church."

> —Lukas Vischer of the Swiss Reformed Church, addressing the Budapest Assembly on behalf of the World Alliance of Reformed Churches

"Had [Christ] remained in heaven as crown prince basking in the music of the angels, he would still be studying recommendations by Michael and Gabriel, perhaps even counter-recommendations from the fallen angels, pleading the complexity and complications of the tension between East and West, North and South, small and big apartheid, etc. Then a vote would follow . . . simple or two-thirds majority . . . matter shelved . . . or referred to the Holy Spirit . . . to report back to Christ . . . to make further recommendations to the Father, who would take the matter back to the full council . . . and taking into account the outcome of possible meetings scheduled for next year . . . if it does not rain. Had Christ operated from heaven, he would still be there today, and you and I would be assembled in hell, with not the slightest peace and hope. Fortunately, Christ decided. He came. He destroyed apartheid between God and humankind and among humankind by taking the whip into the temple divided into the courts of Gentiles, women, Israel, Holy Place, and Holy of Holies. He drove apartheid and robbery out of the church."

> —Dean T. Simon Farisani of South Africa (Evangelical Lutheran Church in Southern Africa) in presentation to the Budapest Assembly

"We can't talk about Jesus Christ as the hope of the world if we don't want to talk about the evil of apartheid."

> —Zephaniah Kameeta of Namibia (Evangelical Lutheran Church in South-West Africa/Namibia), in statement at Budapest Assembly

For discussion

1. Read the quotations at chapter's beginning and end, reflect on them, and share comments or questions about them.

2. Talk about the kind of Lutheran witness and unity which the group would like to see beyond the nation's borders. How can the Lutheran family best express its transnational character when the churchly authority is vested mostly in national churches?

3. What should be needed for Lutheran churches to accept each other for purposes of full fellowship? Is the LWF doctrinal basis enough? If you would add to it, what would you add?

4. Do you agree with the judgment that apartheid is a heresy—that is, a denial of a central teaching of the Christian faith? Discuss continuing evidences of racial discrimination in the life of your own church, locally and nationally. In the life of your society, locally and nationally.

5. Some of the North American delegates in Budapest were reluctant to vote for suspension of the white southern African churches because of awareness that there is racism also in our churches. Do you believe your congregation has functional barriers to persons of other races? Would your congregation willingly call and receive a pastor of a color other than that which is dominant in its membership?

6. Next Sunday at worship, imagine you are a person of another color, a different religious faith, or economically very poor. Jot down the feelings you might experience during the service and be prepared to share them at the next meeting of the study group.

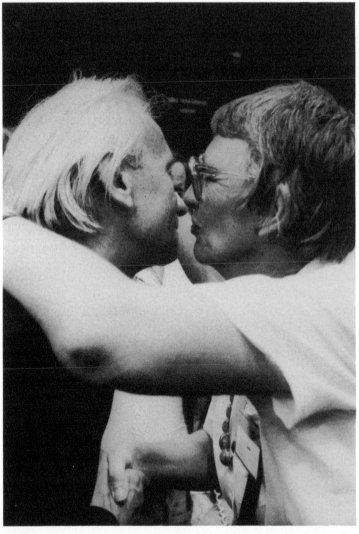

Bishop Kaldy of Hungary is congratulated on his election to the LWF presidency by runner-up Bodil Sølling of Denmark.

6

Who Gives Leadership to the Family?

"Can we be the people of God who accept the historical responsibility for putting an end to talking *about full partnership for women and youth and who start* practicing *the shalom of partnership? To be very specific, which one of the men here will give up his post in the LWF so that a woman can have his position?*

> —*Margaret Wold of the United States, in her presentation on mission at the Budapest Assembly*

"I, your Lord and Teacher, have just washed your feet. You, then, should wash one another's feet. I have set an example for you, so that you will do just what I have done for you."
—*John 13:14-15 TEV*

First a Polish pope! Now a Hungarian leading the world's Lutherans? What does it say that these two large Christian communions are led by eastern Europeans, persons from churches living within social orders shaped by Marxist-Leninist ideology? It may be nothing more than coincidence. Or it may have broad significance.

What is not in doubt is the fact that geography was one of the key concerns as the global family of Lutherans chose its leadership at the Budapest Assembly for the next period of years. Indeed, the question of the categories from which persons should be chosen for leadership in the church was a major one at the Seventh Assembly. Aspects of that question, focused around gender and generation as well as geography, are the subject of this chapter. As we know, these concerns are not limited to the church's international expression.

Why not be blind to demographics?

There is an irony in the concern among Christians these days over the demographic characteristics of persons chosen to represent us. And that irony is one we must be quite clear about. On the one hand, we know that in Christ the differences of gender, age, race, economic class, and all other human distinctions count for absolutely nothing. ("You are all one in Christ Jesus," Gal. 3:28). On the other hand, there is rather compelling evidence from centuries of experience that churches behave much like other human organizations and, unless they intentionally decide to behave otherwise, will give disproportionate authority and leadership responsibility to certain categories of people.

In other words, in order to behave as though we *are* "all one in Christ Jesus" we must structure our family life in a way that ensures fairness to persons from all significant categories of human distinctiveness. That's an irony. It strikes one as contradictory that we must take human distinctions into account in order to get to a point where we can move beyond a preoccupation with human distinctions.

Concern about quotas or proportionate representation is not new in the church. Deliberate attention to geography in the gatherings and decision making of the larger church has been present from the beginning. In more recent centuries, distinguishing between those who are ordained and those who are not has become part of standard governance procedure for Lutheran churches in North America. (It is worth noting that clergy/lay representation has not been truly proportionate, however. When the usual division is 50% ordained–50% unordained, and when clergy in Canadian and U.S. Lutheran churches number only three among every 1000 members, it's clear that a member of the clergy has 333 times as great a chance of being selected as a nonclergy person. We have done better at achieving equity in geographic terms, since delegate seats for regional and national gatherings are almost always apportioned on a basis of membership by geographic subunits.)

What, then, *are* categories of human distinctiveness that truly have significance for church governance? By long tradition, it appears that ordained status and geography are two of them. How many other characteristics which differentiate people are to be used in this matter of selecting the church's leadership? We can probably agree that *some* differences among human beings don't really matter when we select leaders (left- or right-handedness, for instance, or being bald-headed, or whether persons have siblings or are sole children).

Most people would say that recognizing human variations is important only if those variations have been factors in terms of power or advantage or privilege within the church and the larger society in which the church exists. Then the differentiations become significant and primary, and basic justice must take them into account.

Thus, in much of the world today, to be male and of European background still confers certain advantages, almost as a given. In the global church, to be clergy and of middle age also tends to be advantageous in offering opportunities for leadership. The argument of those seeking to change the traditional patterns of governance is that intentional provision for representation from other categories must be made or else it won't happen. The evidence of history is strongly on their side. What are the significant categories? Within the churches today, these are the major ones:

1. Gender (women as well as men should be chosen).

2. Generation (persons under 30 and over 65 should be represented).

3. Race/nationality (in a North American setting, persons of other than European background deserve representation; in a global setting, persons from the East and the South do).

There are some other categories which, increasingly, receive attention as significant for representation purposes, such as:

● persons with disabling conditions

● persons living in poverty (some overlap with no. 3, above, especially in the global setting)

Geography as a factor

And so the debate over quotas has become a normal feature of church life in our day, whether we are discussing formation of new churches at the national level or in decisions about the composition of governance bodies at the international level. All parties to the debate agree that it is preferable for equitable representation to occur without quotas, as a matter of routine, random selection of people. But until that happens as a routine, random occurrence— say the advocates of quotas—there should be *intentional* provisions to insure that the underrepresented are included.

Among the least persuasive arguments against such provisions is the one that goes something like this: "Let's trust the Holy Spirit to choose the best persons, without fussing over categories, since there are no categories in Christ Jesus." Such an argument is particularly unpersuasive when offered by a clergy male of European descent who is in his middle years of life.

Like many international organizations, both religious and nonreligious, the Lutheran World Federation historically has turned to the North Atlantic countries (Western and Northern Europe and North America) for its leadership. Every LWF general secretary (chief staff person) and all but one LWF president in its first 37 years of existence came from the North Atlantic region. That was not entirely disproportionate, since three-fourths of the Lutherans in LWF member churches reside in that region.

But when in 1977, for the first time, the Federation turned to another region for its president, choosing Bishop Josiah Kibira of Tanzania, there was strong consensus that it was about time. In anticipation of the next assembly in 1984, voices in eastern European churches were saying it was time for the Lutheran family to choose one of *their* number as its leader. And many in other regions of the world agreed.

The candidate for LWF presidency who came from the East was Bishop Zoltan Kaldy of the Lutheran Church in Hungary. The discussion of the election prior to and during the Assembly centered heavily on his candidacy. Two central questions were raised: (1) Would a president from an eastern European country be able to speak to global issues of justice and peace in an evenhanded way, or would governmental restraints be present? (2) If an eastern European could serve as the kind of free and international voice needed, would Bishop Kaldy be the best choice among eastern European possibilities?

The ballot for president which confronted delegates at Budapest had three other names:

Roger Nostbakken of Canada, theologian and president-elect of Lutheran Theological Seminary, Saskatoon.

David W. Preus of the United States, presiding bishop of The American Lutheran Church.

Bodil Sølling of Denmark, associate general secretary of Danchurchaid, the development and relief agency of the Danish Lutheran Church.

The two leading vote-getters on the first ballot were Kaldy (136) and Sølling (78). On the second ballot Kaldy was elected, 173 to 124.

Kaldy, born in 1919, became a bishop in the Hungarian church in 1958. It was a trying time for the Lutherans and other Christians in Hungary, as they sought to find their appropriate relationship with the government following the 1956 Hungarian uprising. Kaldy was a leader of the effort to fashion a new, nonconfrontational style of relationship with the political order. He has represented Hungarian Lutherans in the national parliament for a number of years. Prior to becoming bishop, Kaldy was pastor and dean of the Lutheran congregation in the city of Pecs in southern Hungary.

He is married to Magdolna Kaldy, a member of the economics faculty in a Marxist university in Budapest; she is an active Christian and not a Marxist.

Bishop Kaldy's church has 430,000 baptized members in some 300 congregations. It is the third largest church in Hungary, after the Roman Catholic and the Reformed. Among Lutheran memberships in eastern Europe, only those of the German Democratic Republic and the Baltic republics of the Soviet Union are larger. The Lutheran Church in Hungary has been a member of LWF from its founding in 1947.

The new president of the world Lutheran family says his special interests include the international peace issue and economic-political questions. In response to a question from a press representative following his election, Bishop Kaldy said:

There are irreconcilable differences between Marxist-Leninist doctrine and Christian teaching. But between *people* [who follow those two doctrines], between *people* of the East and the West, there are no irreconcilable differences.

(A more detailed look at the challenge to the church in various social settings appears in Chapter 8—and Chapter 7 will discuss issues of representation for the churches of the Southern Hemisphere.)

Youth and age

Youth is defined by the Lutheran World Federation as being under 30 years of age. The LWF encouraged member churches to name youth to at least 20% of their delegate spots for the Budapest Assembly. The goal was not quite reached: 57 (18%) of the 320 delegates were under 30.

Those 57 had joined with other youth for eight days just prior to the Assembly in a Pre-Assembly Youth Gathering. Coming from 49 nations, the 300 participants were equally divided between Eastern Europe and the rest of the world. One press observer, Fritz Johner of the Swiss Evangelical Press Service in Zurich, expressed pleasure at "the manner in which these young people from all corners of the world, with their varying cultural and political backgrounds, worked through these problems and with each other: openness and friendliness, straight thinking, tolerance and willingness to listen even to those who think differently, without aggressiveness even during arguments." He concluded:

> The impression stays with you that, even internationally, jumping over cultural and ideological differences, a new feeling of life is beginning to spread among young people, which is leading to new thinking and changed behavior.

The Youth Gathering brought a lengthy list of recommendations to the Assembly. Many of them were incorporated into the proposals from the Assembly working group on youth and society. The major ones adopted by the Assembly (the first four as recommendations to the Executive Committee) are:

1. To continue the guideline for assemblies which asks that at least 20% of all delegates be youth.

2. To continue the youth coordinator position in the LWF, with a consultant on youth concerns from each of six regions to work with the coordinator.

3. To include a youth as a full member of each of the four LWF Commissions.

4. To ask that regional workshops be conducted on renewal of worship life, with special attention to the needs of youth.

5. To ask the LWF Executive Committee to name two youth as consultants to the Committee, with status akin to that of Commission chairpersons.

6. To urge member churches to seek ways of being involved with the International Youth Year declared by the United Nations for 1985.

7. To encourage the LWF and member churches to develop programs relating to youth in mission, including attention to the question of why young people leave the church.

Those who looked with reporter Johner to youth's "new thinking and changed behavior" suffered a disappointment when the Assembly failed to include a single youth among the 30 members it elected to the Executive Committee which will lead the LWF during the next seven years. The Assembly subsequently asked the Executive Committee to evaluate the question of representation, with special attention given to the presence of youth, and to bring recommendations to the next assembly.

It was noted by all participants at Budapest that the Assembly proceedings departed only twice from planned, scheduled activity. One of the few eruptions into spontaneity came at the conclusion to the evening session in which the Youth Gathering made its report. For nearly an hour, all Assembly participants were pulled from their seats into a human chain which danced and weaved its way through the rows of tables and chairs. For those minutes the plenary hall became a sea of movement, color, and music. The two weeks of Assembly business would have benefited from more such spontaneous celebration. (The other was a demonstration by women at the opening of one session).

The contribution of youth also included a special prayer vigil which focused on world hunger (see Chapter 7). A Swedish youth singing group named *Fjedur* animated the Assembly. And, in addition to actions already noted, recommendations from youth as delegates and from the Pre-Assembly Youth Gathering worked their way into the other reports of Assembly working groups.

Women organize

The most dramatic steps taken by the Seventh Assembly toward greater inclusiveness were in participation by women. To begin with, the Budapest delegates included a higher proportion of women than any previous LWF Assembly: 32.3% compared to 24.5% at the 1977 Assembly in Dar es Salaam.

The increased role of women was most visible in the emergence of Bodil Sølling as a candidate for president. The fact that she became the chief challenger to Bishop Kaldy suggests that future assemblies will likely also give serious consideration to candidates who are neither ordained nor male.

The Assembly did not elect a woman as president, but it took specific actions designed to assure a larger future role for women in the affairs of the global Lutheran family.

1. It asked the Executive Committee seriously to consider implementing a representation plan which would

place at least 40% women and 40% men on all LWF governance structures. (The same recommendation calls for a minimum representation of 40% lay and 40% clergy.) If the plan is enacted by the Executive Committee, as expected, the next Assembly will see women occupying not less than 40% of the delegate seats. Further, the executive committee elected by the next Assembly will need to include at least 12 women among its 30 members, compared to the present seven.[1]

2. It asked the Executive Committee to "exert effort" toward the goal that women serve in half the program and supervisory positions on the LWF staff.

In other actions related to the partnership of women and men, the Assembly asked the LWF and member churches:

● to conduct research and offer education in "sexism as a special question of anthropology and Christian ethics";

● "to recognize the violence to women caused by [church] structures, theological teachings, use of language, and at times silence";

● "to help members of the Christian community to express feelings of anger, anxiety, depression in forms other than violence, remembering the human rights of individuals in personal relationships";

● to help members of the Christian community to express concern about "other forms of violence, such as those manifested toward preborn children and women in abortion, remembering the dignity of all human life";

● to be advocates for victims of personal/family violence, providing sanctuary, legal protection, counseling, and economic assistance, and to work actively for just laws for victims of such violence.

Women as church workers

The Assembly also addressed the question of ordination of women. It asked two things:

1. That member churches which do not ordain women give consideration to doing so.

2. That member churches which do ordain women develop policies that insure equality in opportunities for service and in benefits.

A 1980 study by the LWF indicated that only two-fifths of the member churches were then ordaining women. Since most of the larger churches do, however, it is estimated that 80% of the world's Lutherans belong to churches which ordain women. Recent LWF reports point out that Lutheran churches currently reflect five distinct realities on the question of women's ordination:[2]

• Women are ordained and exercise the pastoral ministry with general acceptance and no special conditions.

• Women are ordained, but parts of the church (certain bishops or regional jurisdictions) do not accept female pastors.

• Women are ordained, but special conditions are attached, including required celibacy, local acceptance factors, and restrictions regarding positions ordained women may hold in the church.

• Women are not ordained, and the church has taken an official decision against it.

• Women are not ordained, and the church has taken no position because serious discussion of the question has barely begun.

One of the LWF reports[3] argues that women are welcomed to church employment virtually everywhere and that considerably more than 50% of all church workers are women. "But that does not change the fact that major decision-making is in the hands of men," it says.[4]

Treatment of women by the churches, including ordination, remains one of the questions on which different parts of the Lutheran world family disagree. The Budapest Assembly provided a strong impetus toward open consideration of justice for women within the church's life and

Delegates and other women at the Assembly joined in a demonstration calling for full participation of women in the LWF.

work. In its own organizational life, the LWF itself is being reshaped in the direction of greater equality of the two sexes. Much remains to be done in the member churches themselves, which means there is a great deal of opportunity for those churches to witness to and learn from each other.

The basic challenge was expressed most directly by Margaret Wold of the United States in her Budapest address on mission. Alluding to the LWF 1977 declaration that discrimination on the basis of race is a denial of the Christian confession of faith, she asked, "Should ecclesiastical discrimination against women be declared *status confessionis*?"

Dr. Wold's question was not answered in Budapest. It is one which will continue to occupy a high place on the Lutheran family agenda. However we finally answer it, the question will not go away until the family addresses it openly and boldly.

Words to ponder

"This Assembly [meeting in Budapest] may give a real good service to the small churches, to the Lutherans living in a diaspora situation, to strengthen them in their faith and love and to grow in self-respect in finding their identity: that they belong to the great family of Lutheranism in the world."

> —Bishop Zoltan Kaldy of the Lutheran Church in Hungary, in his July 1980 invitation to the LWF to hold its 1984 Assembly in Budapest

"We ask the LWF Assembly to listen to the heard and unheard cries of young people at least as attentively as [to] anxieties about the existence of the church."

> —Report of Pre-Assembly Youth Gathering to Budapest Assembly

"It is not fair to ask women to spend all their time working to get *into* the system when they could be working *within* the system."

> —Christine Grumm, delegate from the Association of Evangelical Lutheran Churches (U.S.) in debate at Budapest Assembly on representation of women and men in LWF structures

"How can we [member churches of the LWF] be in full fellowship with each other when ordained women from some churches are not welcome at every pulpit? We consider racial discrimination a sin against God. When will we consider discrimination against women as likewise sinful?"

> —Karin Oljelund, delegate from the Church of Sweden, in a speech from the floor at the Budapest Assembly

For discussion

1. Read the quotations at chapter's beginning and end, reflect on them, and share comments or questions about them.

2. How do you feel about the legitimacy of proportionate representation in the church's decision-making processes for persons of various demographic categories? Is it proper for any such distinctions to be considered? If so, which of these should be recognized (for regional/national/international structures): ordained/unordained status? geography? gender? generation? ethnic background?

3. Do you feel a person who lives under a government that is officially atheist must necessarily be limited as a spokesperson for an international church organization? Why or why not? Do leaders from capitalist countries have any limitations placed on them by their cultures?

4. Are the reasons people give for opposing ordination of women primarily theological or primarily ones of cultural habit? Can the two become intermixed?

5. How does the group feel about Margaret Wold's suggestion that discrimination against women by the church must be opposed on the basis of the faith itself? (See Chapter 5 for discussion of *status confessionis* in relation to apartheid.)

7

How Shall the Family Live Amid Poverty and Wealth?

'' . . . since you have plenty at this time, it is only fair that you should help those who are in need. Then, when you are in need and they have plenty, they will help you. In this way, both are treated equally.''
    —*2 Corinthians 8:13-14 TEV*

''It is impossible only to celebrate and to stay out of politics, as long as people suffer.''
    —*Report of Pre-Assembly Youth Gathering to Budapest Assembly*

It is often the case at international church gatherings that participants recess from passionate discussion of global poverty and hunger to meal breaks marked by embarrassingly opulent quantities and varieties of food and drink. It happened again at the Budapest Assembly of the Lutheran World Federation.

As is also commonly the case, it was the *youth* participants who called attention to the contradiction between words and behavior. At Budapest, toward the end of the Assembly, they organized a through-the-night vigil to which all Assembly participants were invited. On the day

Martha Ahmadou of Cameroon read Scripture during an Assembly worship service.

preceding the vigil, participants were encouraged by the youth to skip either or both of the two main meals and to turn in their meal tickets. The Assembly also arranged for the lunch served that day, even for those who ate, to be more modest. In all, the reduction and elimination of meals netted a total equivalent to $15,000 in U.S. currency which the LWF agreed to designate for immediate aid to victims of drought in Zimbabwe.

The efforts of youth in arranging for the one-day fast and the night-long vigil helped Assembly participants to think about the relationship between the words spoken by world church meetings and the consumption-heavy life-style lived by those same meetings. The Assembly also took several significant actions advocating changes in the future behavior of the Federation, its member churches, and the national governments of the world—all seeking to address the gulf between the poor and the rich of this planet.

Representation—south and north

Within the Lutheran family itself there is an economic division which cannot be hidden. Most of the member churches of the Northern Hemisphere are located in countries of great wealth, and most of the baptized in those churches live in at least economic comfort, some in genuine affluence. The member churches of the Southern Hemisphere, by contrast, with few exceptions live in societies which are impoverished. How should the family address such inequities, both those within the Lutheran fellowship and those within the larger planetary setting?

One way the gap is addressed is by looking at the question of representation. Do the people and the churches of the low-income world have a fair share of the votes and the leadership within the family? In answering that question, a brief historical review will be helpful.

At the first assembly of the LWF (Lund, 1947), 92% of the delegates came from the Northern Hemisphere. Of the 8% from the South, half were northern-world missionaries; thus only one delegate in 25 was indigenous to the low-income regions of the planet.

By the time of the Seventh Assembly in Budapest, 58% of the member churches and 15% of the membership of the LWF were located in the South. (Because many of the southern churches are small, their proportion of baptized

Lutherans among the Federation churches is much lower than their share of the member churches.) At Budapest, churches of the South had 40% of the delegates—more than their proportion of baptized Lutherans, but less than their share of the member churches. Each member church, no matter how small, is entitled to at least one delegate. Southern churches also have 37% of the seats on the 30-member LWF executive committee.

There were proposals at Budapest to increase the South's share of representation on all LWF governing bodies and among executive staff to 50%. Delegates defeated that move, apparently feeling that the present proportions are fair. They voted that leadership positions within LWF governance bodies should insure representation for churches of the South "at least by a percentage equal to their membership."

The Assembly also changed the LWF constitution so that each of six regions (Africa, Asia, Latin America, North America, Eastern Europe, Western Europe) will always be represented by either the president or one of five vice-presidents. Thus, the southern churches now are assured 50% of the seats on the LWF's six-member presidium.

Advocacy with national governments

The Assembly asked member churches to urge two actions upon their national governments, in an effort to begin closing the gap between rich nations and poor nations.

First, governments of the industrialized nations of the North should be asked to "set aside at least 1% of their gross national product" for economic assistance to low-income countries. Among the few which have attained that level of development assistance are the largely Lutheran nations of Norway and Sweden. The Netherlands is another. The current Canadian proportion is 0.47% of GNP. For the United States it is 0.24%.[1] Governments of the Soviet Union and the eastern bloc countries do not publish comparable figures, but their levels of economic aid to low-income nations are believed to be far below the 1% goal.

Second, member churches in all countries should urge their governments to redirect 1% of their military budget to emergency aid for drought victims, especially in Africa, and to inform the LWF general secretary of actions the member churches take in this regard. (For the United States in 1985, 1% of the military budget amounts to $3 billion in U.S. currency; for Canada it equals $70 million Canadian.)

The Assembly also adopted a proposal submitted jointly by two working groups: those dealing with Caring for God's Creation and with Economic and Social Justice. The recommendation asks that LWF initiate a long-term study of models of economic order which do not depend on continuous growth in production and consumption. The study should be done using consultants drawn from the LWF member churches, the Roman Catholic church, the World Council of Churches, and other religious bodies, and the results are to be shared with the member churches.

Economic gap threatens peace

Following an action of the Dar es Salaam Assembly, the LWF World Service Department in 1978 established an Office of Research and Social Action, giving it the task of helping member churches to study the root causes of social and economic injustice. That office also relates to such United Nations agencies as the UN Conference on Trade and Development and urges the member churches to advocate for more justice in trade among the nations.[2]

In its comprehensive report to the Assembly the working group on Social and Economic Justice stated that "the growing gap between rich and poor is an increasing threat to peace and survival, and a violation of the Gospel." The working group noted that the poor of the earth always

Delegates voted with red cards to facilitate counting during Seventh Assembly sessions.

live by hope: "Hope for an end to suffering, hope for justice," and added that the believers among them subsume those hopes within their overall hope in Jesus Christ.

Among the recommendations from the Social/Economic Justice working group which the Assembly adopted were these:

1. That the LWF executive committee ask the member churches:
● to examine the Scriptures with greater attention in teaching, preaching, and worship to the call to "set at liberty those who are oppressed, to seek justice, and to be a church in solidarity with the poor";
● to work with member churches in other countries in conducting studies on global economic issues, specifically "those related to commodity prices and the expanding power of transnational corporations";
● to examine the relationship of "their fund-raising efforts to development education and advocacy," reminding their members that Christians are called to practice both charity and justice;
● to influence their governments, especially in the industrialized countries, "to shift resources from military to

peaceful uses, to offer fair rates of currency exchange, to [seek] effective measures to lower interest rates . . . and to [negotiate with the low-income countries] with the aim of establishing an equitable international monetary, financial, and commodity-pricing system";

● to withdraw investments from business entities "doing business with South Africa";

● "to survey their resources, including assets and income, and develop a plan for just, equitable sharing of those resources among the member churches," such a plan to be presented at the Eighth Assembly;

● to use such vehicles as the Ecumenical Development Cooperative Society "as a channel for investment funds for development projects initiated by the poor";

● to "affirm and support people in poor and rich nations who face intimidation and oppression as they work for justice in church and society."

2. That the LWF Commission on World Service be asked:

● to strengthen its service to member churches through its Office for Research and Social Action (ORSA), helping the churches to conduct programs of development education and action related to root causes of economic and social injustice;

● to work with the member churches toward a possible Special Consultation on North-South Issues, which would seek a strategy for "radical changes in the world's economic systems" as resolved by the 1977 LWF Assembly;

● to provide scholarship help to encourage in member churches "local self-study and analysis as well as study of issues related to the New International Economic Order."

3. That the LWF executive committee consider asking:

● that all new activities of LWF include a concern for root causes of social/economic injustice in their planning, implementation, impact, and evaluation, and that for the next period LWF budget and staffing reflect "a significantly greater financial commitment to attacking the root causes of injustice";

● that member churches urge their national governments to strengthen their support for agencies such as the UN Conference on Trade and Development, the UN Food and Agriculture Organization, and the World Food Council.

To combat hunger and poverty . . .

With specific reference to the LWF's own work among low-income people, the Assembly took several actions. First, a constitutional change added to the purpose of the World Service Department these words: " . . . to help Lutheran churches and groups as a sharing community to serve human need and to promote social and economic justice." The department then was asked in its development activities to:

1. Place more emphasis on elements of agricultural systems beyond the growing of food, such as local marketing and distribution, fair wages for rural workers, formation of cooperatives, and assistance to systems for local consumption rather than export of food.

2. Continue through its Community Development Service to help churches in their ministries with the poor and suffering, including awareness building and advocacy.

3. Emphasize the particular involvement of women in the planning, leadership, and implementation of development programs, as well as addressing their special needs in situations of poverty and hunger.

4. Seek ways for more meaningful involvement by youth in development programs.

5. Stress the needs of people displaced in their own countries by war or other civil unrest, since intergovernmental agencies such as the United Nations are not able to meet their needs effectively. World Service was also urged to increase its work in refugee assistance generally, both in immediate aid and in programs leading to self-reliance or voluntary repatriation.

The Assembly noted that LWF World Service "has a considerable and internationally recognized experience" in work with refugees. It is especially noteworthy in Africa, and LWF has been exploring ways of bringing its refugee expertise to other areas of the world, such as Central America.

Finally, the Assembly commended World Service for its work with Roman Catholics and other Protestant agencies in the Churches' Drought Action in Africa and urged the member churches "to continue to support this unique ecumenical action aimed at reducing the specter of mass starvation in Africa during the coming years."

Who's aiding whom?

When the subject is the closing of the gap between rich and poor, it is easy to envision a flow of resources in one direction only: from the North to the South, from the high-income to the low-income countries and churches. That image is incomplete, however. There is more to it than a simple North to South flow.

First, there is a growing stream of resource exchange *within* the South: from the churches of low-income countries to other churches of low-income countries. It is a transfer of ideas and experiences and personnel more than a transfer of economic resources, though some of that is happening also. An international organization like the Lutheran World Federation is ideally equipped to help facilitate such a South to South exchange. For example, its Community Development Service recently sent a team of water drilling experts from India to Ethiopia.

Second, there is a growing flow from South to North as well. Whenever the South's churches send spokespersons to the North to educate the Christians there about the economic and political shape of the world as seen from its underside—then there is aid flowing from South to North! Whenever the churches of the South send personnel as pastors, as teachers, even as students to the northern countries—then there is aid from South to North! Whenever the churches of the South nurture their northern counterparts with zeal for evangelizing our post-Christian neighbors, with their passion for a hope-filled future, with their faith in a God who suffers with human beings—then there is aid flowing from South to North! (Further, whenever the countries of the South send to the North the willing hands of people— whether they are farm workers or physicians—then there is aid flowing from South to North!)

It may be, as long as the economic resources are skewed so heavily to the northern half of the planet, that the material poverty of the South must be addressed through more sharing and structural changes on the part of the North. But it is certainly true also that the *spiritual* poverty of the North in our time needs all the help it can get from the riches of the churches and the cultures of the South. *Each* half of the family has oppressions from which it needs to be liberated. *Each* half of the family needs the other half for help with that liberation. That's precisely what the family of God is for.

(For related thoughts on the flows of aid, see comments by Altmann and Fuliga under ''Words to Ponder'' at close of this chapter.)

North-south intersects with east-west

It was said repeatedly at Budapest: we can't talk about peace without talking about justice . . . we can't view the world's problems and fears along either a North-South axis or an East-West axis, but must learn to view both ways simultaneously. As it was phrased by Margareta Grape-Lantz of Sweden:

> We must understand that poverty in the Third World is not exclusively the result of later development. It is also a serious consequence of the way the rich part of the world is organized, both economically and politically. The poor are

not only justified in demanding justice within their countries. The injustice they suffer also constitutes a vital threat to the survival of everybody on earth.[3]

Thus, peace and justice are tied together, and the biblical theme of *shalom* (the harmony or wholeness that is a combination of justice and peace) looms into our consciousness. And therefore the subjects of Chapters 7 and 8 in this book are appropriately back to back.

Words to ponder

"The worsening economic situation in the world and the severe drought in Africa have affected women seriously. For some this has meant going hungry and watching helplessly as their children are dying a slow death from starvation. They struggle to survive and to keep their families together with the very minimum of basic needs and often none. To have a second dress for some women is a luxury. Yet they continue to hope for a better future."

—Kaanaeli Makundi of Tanzania in a statement to the Budapest Assembly

"Am I mistaken in thinking that in spite of everything there is more hope today in the Third World than in the developed capitalist and socialist countries? Could it not be that abundance, power, and armaments produce— more than anything else—emptiness, fear, and despair? Meanwhile, hopes are germinating in the Third World, and these include hope for the renewal and growth of the churches. . . . It may be impossible to sustain the conviction that hopes come from the East and the West. . . . "

—Walter Altmann of Brazil in a presentation on justice at the Budapest Assembly

"The churches in the South are struggling out of their captivity to the traditions, policies, theological expressions, liturgies, and structures they have been taught. They realize that some of these are irrelevant to their needs and situations. But many of them don't know of alternatives because they have not been given the opportunity to learn from fellow churches in the South."

—Dean José B. Fuliga of the Lutheran Theological Seminary in the Philippines, in a presentation on mission at the Seventh Assembly

"The last seven years have brought some awakening, development of skills, and raising of status for women in India and Asia. We have been awakened from the traditional shyness and backwardness, moving slowly from passivity to action, from silence to speech, and from mere work to participation. Our culture, in which women are looked upon as a financial drain, has left many of us with feelings of guilt and low self-esteem. The affirmation of our womanhood is restoring self-worth to our women. The realization that women have more to offer to the church and society than child-bearing and house-keeping has lifted our spirits and raised our horizons and our hopes."

—Katakshamma Paul Raj of India, in a statement to the Budapest Assembly

"The industrial nations have developed their economies and amassed vast riches, mainly at the expense of the undeveloped nations. They have for generations acquired the raw materials produced by these peoples at minimal prices and sold them finished goods made . . . from these materials at many times their original prices. This process is still continuing and has produced imbalance and resentment that threaten to explode into open hostility. . . . The nations that are piling wealth at the expense of the less developed nations will surely pay up sooner or later, for it is impossible that people should live on the same planet for long, half rich and half poor, half overfed and half starving."

> —Emmanuel Abraham of Ethiopia, in presentation on caring for creation at Budapest Assembly

For discussion

1. Read the quotations at the beginning and end of the chapter, reflect on them, and share comments or questions about them.

2. Why do certain nations of the Western industrialized community do so much better than others when it comes to sharing with the poor countries in economic assistance? (The figures given in this chapter and in note 1 are official or governmental aid—if voluntary giving were included the U.S. proportion would increase to about 0.3%. Also, military aid is not included.)

3. How do you feel about the suggestion that the LWF churches examine their assets and incomes and develop a plan for "just, equitable sharing of those resources among the member churches"?

4. Our congregations have learned how to resettle refugees from many parts of the world, becoming quite proficient at this ministry. How might we become more involved in addressing the problems that *create* refugees in the first place? What do you think the causes are? What can we together, through our churches, do about those causes?

5. Discuss the aid which the churches (and countries) of the North need to receive from the churches (and countries) of the South. Can members of the group point to examples of it in their own communities?

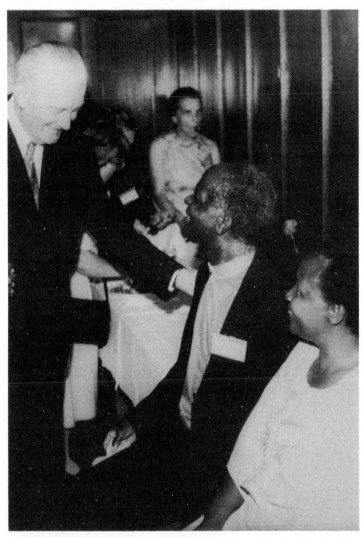

Janos Kádár, top leader of the Hungarian government, greeted Bishop Josiah Kibira, retiring LWF president, at a government reception for world Lutheran leaders.

8

How Shall the Family Work for Peace in the World?

"We must find the theology that fits our time and place. Liberation theology cannot be transferred to Hungary, nor the Hungarian theology of diakonia to Latin America."

> —*participant in working group on Differing Social Systems, Budapest Assembly*

"Hope is the capacity to live with danger without being overwhelmed by it; hope is the will to struggle against obstacles even when they appear insuperable."

> —*Pastoral Letter of the U.S. Roman Catholic Bishops on War and Peace, 1983*

George Kennan, former United States ambassador to the Soviet Union, wrote in 1981:

This entire preoccupation with nuclear war is a form of illness. . . . There is no hope in it—only horror. It can be understood only as some form of sub-conscious despair on the part of its devotees—some sort of death wish, a readiness to commit suicide for fear of death . . . a lack of faith, or better a lack of the very strength that it takes to have faith, as countless of our generations have had it before us.[1]

If plans for fighting with nuclear weapons are devoid of hope, where does that leave the human race today? Studies among children in various countries reveal that many of them do indeed lack long-term hope, have little expectation of living to old age, and believe their parents' and grandparents' generations are helpless to divert the world from its dash toward nuclear death.

What have the churches to say in the face of such a vacuum of hope? In particular, what have Lutherans to say? Lutherans who, as much as any of the world's faith families, have strength on both sides of the East-West divide! Lutherans, who had a family gathering in 1984 under the theme "In Christ—*Hope* for the World!"

Christians in differing social systems

One word that can be spoken from Lutheran experience is that the church can live and bring a message of hope under a variety of social systems. The Budapest Assembly devoted a major amount of attention to that subject. Its working group on Christian Life in Different Social Systems observed that, while the church of Christ transcends all national, economic, and cultural boundaries, still there "are problems in mutual understanding within and between churches of the North and South, East and West."

A common assumption in the churches outside the eastern bloc (nations dominated by the Soviet Union) is that the churches in the East are so controlled by their governments that they are unable fully to be the church. The response to that analysis, voiced consistently by delegates from the churches of Eastern Europe at the Budapest Assembly, ran essentially like this: "Yes, we *are* strongly shaped by the forces of our social/political/cultural setting.

But so are your churches in the West and the South, except that you don't usually recognize it."

One member of the working group on Different Social Systems put it this way: "I have yet to find a church anywhere, or at any time in history, which is free of captivity to its culture."

The question of the church's relationship to the human culture in which it is called to live and to serve can be subdivided into several questions. Among them are these:

● Would it be wise for the church to be totally free of its culture, even if that were possible? Must the church always seek to be *counter*cultural, in every respect?

● How can the church truly be *in* the culture, but not *of* the culture? How does it speak and live a message from outside human wisdom (the gospel) and yet make that message credible to human beings who are always shaped by particular human cultures?

● How can the various national churches help each other, across national boundaries, to see the culture-captivity of each?

It ought to be transparently clear that one reason the national churches of the global Christian family need each other is that we all tend to be blind to certain realities until someone from outside our own setting comes and points out those things that have been hidden to us. The churches of the LWF family have benefited from such outside viewing in many instances. Two examples are the several "Mission on Six Continents" visits which went to various national church settings in the 1970s and the Japanese Lutheran peace team which visited the U.S. and Canadian churches in the spring of 1984.

When churches adapt

One of the lessons of church history is that the Christian movement has always adapted in one way or another to the varieties of political and cultural realities in which it has found itself. Sometimes that adaptation has been courageous, sometimes cowardly. Sometimes (we conclude from the safe perspective of history) it appears to have been appropriate and sometimes not. It is apparent that the churches of today have also adapted to their social settings. Those in the West, it is often charged, have made peace with economic values which prize private acquisition and personal consumption (far too highly). Those in the East, say their critics, have made peace with governments which deny them the freedom to enter political debate in their own societies.

Because the Seventh Assembly was meeting in one of the eastern countries and because a leader of the Hungarian Lutheran Church was a candidate for the LWF presidency, there was much discussion in Budapest of churchly adaptation to social systems. The Hungarian Lutherans have developed a thoughtful analysis of their situation within Hungarian society and what it means for that church's social role. As the host church for the Assembly, they were eager to share their self-understanding with the other members of the family who came to meet in their country.

It began with a confession of sin for past failure. "We no longer live as an elite within our society, with the many privileges that status provided. We now live as believers among unbelievers. This change has not been easy for us, but it has been refreshing for us. We have had to learn how to be the church in our situation, and we have rejected four possibilities." The four ways they decided not to be the church, said the Hungarian Lutherans, are these:

1. Not as a church that is rich and privileged, allied with those who run the society.

2. Not as a church identified with one political party or another.

3. Not by assimilating, so that the church is indistinguishable from the culture as a whole.

4. Not as a ghetto church, withdrawing from any responsibility in society.

"We have had to learn a fifth way," said the Hungarian Lutherans: "the way of confessing Christ as a servant church." The Hungarians have developed a "theology of diakonia"[2] or servanthood. It is characterized by an emphasis on the church's role of providing services in the social order which are permitted by the government, such as care for the elderly and the mentally retarded. It also means basic affirmation of the socialist ordering of the society. This theological approach certainly does not ignore the profound differences between the gospel and the ideology of Marxism-Leninism. It does, however, appear to downplay the church's prophetic role within its own society. There seems to be little place for the church to advocate alternatives within the Hungarian social order.

Thus, the critics of the theology of diakonia point out that the sin which the Hungarian Lutherans say they committed in the old order—failure to speak the critical, public, prophetic word—is being repeated in today's new order as well.

One of the problems for those who would criticize another church's way of being the church is that we follow a human tendency of wanting to change the other person but not ourselves. We in the West are usually more ready to support changes in the churches and the societies of the East than in our own churches and nations. We have not had the experience of seeking to be the church under political ideologies which are formally anti-God and which claim to be supreme in all areas of human concern. The Hungarian (and other eastern European) Lutherans need a critique from others in the Lutheran family. But that works both ways. The rest of us need equally to hear what our sisters and brothers in the East (and the South) are saying to us about *our* cultural captivity, *our* blind spots, *our* failures to be faithful. In other words, across national and cultural divides, we need each other; we need to be loving critics for each other.

Help across the borders

The Assembly in Budapest addressed to the Executive Committee several recommendations from its working group on Different Social Systems. Among them are these:

1. That continuation and expansion of Christian-Marxist dialogue by the churches both within and between nations be strongly encouraged.

2. That the LWF help member churches in the so-called Christian countries, particularly the national churches as in Scandinavia, to study how to encounter secularization and the rise of new religions.

3. That the LWF study on civil religion be continued.

4. That exchange visits between member churches be given "every possible priority" as a way of helping Lutherans understand life in various social systems.

5. That the member churches continue seeking to proclaim the gospel in every cultural context, "without losing its true, unique, and universal content or eliminating the possibility of a true cross-cultural theological dialogue. . . ."

6. That member churches be urged to develop Bible studies showing "the connection between the cross and cross-cultural relationships."

7. That the LWF provide studies on different social systems for addressing people at grass-roots levels, in many languages, and offer consulting services to the churches "concerning their role of advocacy and their prophetic witness."

The working group report underscored the need for member churches to engage in "sympathetic communication [with one another], to gain knowledge about each other, to recognize each other as Christians, and to co-operate and dialogue with one another in order to report on their work, experiences, and challenges to one another."

And on international peace?

Another group at Budapest worked on the question of international tensions and especially the threat of nuclear war. In the working group's discussion, one participant argued that, "On the one hand, Christians move into work for peace from the distinctive emphasis of the reconciliation of all humankind in Christ. But on the other hand, Christians dare not act exclusively, as though they alone have the answers. Others move into peace work from different experiences, for example, the Japanese experience of atomic terror."

Thus, believers and nonbelievers must work together for peace. And yet the churches have special gifts and resources to contribute to that work. What are they?

First, said the Assembly in its official statement on peace, Christians begin with the conviction that "Christ is the servant of peace, bringing reconciliation between God and humankind, calling us as his followers to serve him also in building peace and justice." Gunnar Staalsett[3] of Norway, a participant in the peace working group discussion, pointed the group to what he called the rediscovery of peace and justice as a major biblical theme:

> In past centuries the church rediscovered global mission and diakonia, and saw that they were implicit in every biblical page. In our period of the church's life, we are rediscovering peace and justice on every page of the Bible.

Further, the Assembly noted that in the biblical witness there is no separation between peace and justice. They are linked together because neither can exist without the other. "There can be no lasting peace as long as people starve, injustices prevail, or people are oppressed, persecuted, or discriminated against because of their faith, view of life, race, sex, or ethnic origin. Social and economic injustice as well as ideological conflicts are at the roots of many of the wars of liberation. . . . To accept the prevailing unjust situation in many parts of the world, particularly in the so-called Third World, is a denial of peace."

On the present nuclear dilemma, the report said that "no use of nuclear arms can be morally justified." It also said, "another basis than the deterrence system has to be found for a stable relationship among the major military alliances."

Peace actions: the member churches

Among the recommendations to the member churches adopted by the Budapest Assembly were these:

1. Encourage congregations in untiring attention to global peace and justice through proclamation, prayer, education, and pastoral care.

2. Study anew the theological and ethical bases for ministries of peace and teach the faith's imperatives for peace/justice to all age groups, with specific training in peace ministries provided for church workers.

3. Plan and implement annual times for special focus on global peace/justice.

4. Facilitate exchange among congregations across ideological, national, socio-economic, and confessional boundaries.

5. Urge their governments to work toward "replacing the system of deterrence with a negotiated system of global security through step-by-step, verifiable, mutual reductions of both nuclear and conventional weapons arsenals."

6. Ask governments to "strengthen education toward peace and confidence-building, to abandon education toward hatred, and to separate pre-military training from public education."

7. Oppose discrimination against those who refuse to bear arms for reasons of faith and conscience and urge their governments to permit nonmilitary service and to give them legal recognition.

The Assembly also addressed several recommendations on peace work to the member churches and the LWF jointly:

1. Urge governments of the industrialized nations, both East and West, "to place renewed emphasis on concerns expressed under the concept of the New International Economic Order"—the call from the low-income nations for a restructuring of the global system of economic arrangements.

2. Urge governments of the United States and the Soviet Union "immediately to resume negotiations with the aim of removing medium-range missiles in East and West" and ask all governments to halt research, testing, and production of all weapons for mass annihilation.

3. Appeal to governments and international organizations to work for (*a*) a verifiable nuclear test ban treaty; (*b*) strengthening of the Non-Proliferation Treaty; (*c*) international agreements banning the production and use of nuclear weapons and opposing the militarization of outer space; (*d*) international regulation of the arms trade.

4. Urge their respective governments to speed the negotiations now under way to seek a European Conference on Disarmament.

5. Oppose the use of both economic pressures and military intervention in the affairs of other nations, especially by the superpowers.

6. Urge the governments that are party to military conflicts anywhere in the world to negotiate nonmilitary resolutions.

The role of LWF

The Assembly also saw a particular role for the Lutheran World Federation in the churches' work for peace. It asked that the Executive Committee:

- Establish a special desk for peace concerns, which should:
  a) organize studies on ways of strengthening international law as a means for peaceful conflict resolution;
  b) collect, develop, and circulate resources for congregational peace activity in worship, prayer, and education;
  c) explore the possibility of ecumenical agreement on a special annual time of prayer for peace and justice.
- Provide information to the member churches for exchange and contacts between congregations living in different social systems.

It is apparent that many people see a central role for LWF in helping different parts of the Lutheran family to make contacts across international borders, especially those dividing East and West. The new president, Bishop Kaldy of Hungary, said following his election that he wished to increase the dialog between East and West during his term. He also said it would be one of his goals to work toward an increase in the number of LWF staff who come from churches in Eastern Europe.

Other eastern European church leaders said they welcomed the idea of more contact with Lutherans from outside their region. One said the church in his country was eager for visiting groups from other Lutheran churches, "but we may not be able to return the visits during our lifetime." He also pointed out that "this very good program" of visits and other contacts between congregation members "can be entered only with very conscious awareness of the differing situations in eastern European societies."

On the related matter of respect for human rights, the Assembly in an official statement:

● urged the member churches to intensify their efforts in study and action, working with ecumenical and other international agencies;

● asked member churches to encourage support by their governments of the proposed United Nations International Covenant Against Torture, including its protocol permitting the inspection of prisoners;

● encouraged the LWF Studies Department to develop education aids on human rights for use by the churches.

Special Regional Concerns

Concerns with conflicts in specific regions were also on the Budapest Assembly agenda.

On *Central America*, the Assembly voted to:

1. Direct the general secretary to advocate for the ending of aggression against Nicaragua and El Salvador, "to the appropriate authorities."

2. Ask member churches to cooperate in the rebuilding of El Salvador and Nicaragua, and to work for establishment of human rights throughout Central America.

3. Urge member churches to continue providing assistance to the exiled and displaced persons of Central America.

4. Encourage member churches to ask their governments "to support the diplomatic action of the Contadora Group in trying to negotiate peace in Central America."

In a related action, the Assembly referred to the LWF executive committee a proposal that additional languages (such as Spanish) be used along with German, English, and French at the Eighth Assembly.

On *Namibia*, the Assembly voted to:

1. Repeat the call of member churches and the Council of Churches in Namibia for "an urgent and immediate ceasefire between the South-West Africa People's Organization and South Africa" under the terms of United Nations Resolution 435.

2. Ask the member churches and LWF to "be vigilant in resisting South African propaganda and overtures to compromise our confessional rejection of apartheid."

3. Urge continued support for the Namibian churches in their opposition to South African occupation of their country and in their ministry with victims of oppression.

4. Suggest that the executive committee consider organizing an international conference on Namibia, "with the view to making a united representation to the United Nations."

On the *Middle East*, the Assembly voted to:

1. Receive a statement offered by the Evangelical Lutheran Church in Jordan on the worsening situation of Palestinians and their longing for self-determination.

2. Express the Assembly's "sympathetic solidarity with Arab Christians and especially with the Evangelical Lutheran Church of Jordan."

The fears about the state of the world brought before the Assembly in Budapest were many. The delegates tried to address those fears—with the best of human creativity, to be sure.

But always they returned to the reminder, as their final message to the churches put it, that "Christian hope is not founded in our own strength; it is grounded on the acts of God. . . . We, and all in Christian congregations everywhere, have the privilege of being children of hope."

It is as children of hope that all members of the family are given the strength to live and to serve in times like ours.

Words to ponder

"If Christ were to appear among us today and to ask us, 'Have you done what I told you?', only the nonviolent could respond, 'Yes, Lord!' The rest of us would have to confess: 'Lord, we were too weak. We wanted to prevent evil by means that are effective in the real world.' To that Christ would reply: 'If you had had the courage to venture the way of nonviolence, you would have discovered that it is viable.' I admit I am one of those who have tried to work with the means that are effective in this world. I have not considered governments that depend on electoral majorities . . . to be capable of renouncing violence, and I have tried to find possible ways for such governments to . . . prevent war."

> —Carl Friedrich von Weizsaecker, West German nuclear physicist and peace researcher, in address on peace to the Budapest Assembly

"There is hope for humankind—but only if it does not passively accept the present rather grim situation but instead works actively for global change."

> —Minály Simai, deputy director of the Hungarian Institute for the World Economy, in response to von Weizsaecker address

"The cross is our only hope and the only hope for the world. As Christians, we have to live on the point of intersection between the imperfection of this world and the principles of the Kingdom of God. . . . We know that the Kingdom will never be fully implemented on earth. But we still have to measure society and political systems against the principles of the Kingdom. . . . Brothers and sisters: Is it not fantastic that we, as Christians and far from perfect, have still the mission to reveal some of the mysteries of the Kingdom of God to humankind, to make the invisible visible, to make people see and taste the risen Christ?''

> —Margareta Grape-Lantz, deputy general secretary of the International Center of the Swedish Labor Movement, in response to von Weizsaecker address

''It will be one of our [the LWF member churches'] important challenges to address the tensions between East and West in a constructive way.

> —Roger Nostbakken of Canada, candidate for LWF presidency, replying to a reporter's question on the task of the next period in the LWF's life

''I do not understand this sharp distinction between 'atheist' and 'Christian' states. The United States is certainly not behaving in a Christian way in its current policies.''

> —Janusz Narzynski, bishop of the Evangelical Church of the Augsburg Confession in Poland, in a discussion of the church in various social systems, Budapest Assembly

''It is no secret that some see the root causes for the suffering of the churches in [countries with communist governments] as a lack of participation by earlier generations of Christians in the social transformation of their societies. Others believe that socialist ideologies and Christianity are totally incompatible. May I remind you that Tanzania, where I come from, is a socialist country, with a socialism that has grown out of our own soul. In our country, many of the leaders of the government are professing Christians and Christ is present both in witness and in development work. Maybe this could be a challenge to both East and West to realize how Christ and socialism *can* live together!"

> —Josiah Kibira, retiring president of the LWF, in his opening address at the Budapest Assembly

"Justice and peace have kissed each other."
> —Psalm 85:10 Paraphrased

For discussion

1. Read the quotations at the beginning and end of the chapter, reflect on them, and share comments or questions about them.

2. It is claimed that churches must always, to some degree, reflect their own culture. How can the strengths of that fact be utilized? How can the negative consequences for the gospel be minimized? Do you think your church is more like a mirror, reflecting your culture, or more like salt, seasoning your culture?

3. What are some examples of your church (local, regional, or national) being too much "*of* the culture"?

4. If the system of nuclear deterrence has kept the weapons from being fired in anger for more than three decades, why should that system be criticized as inadequate or immoral? What system for keeping nuclear peace might be put in its place?

5. What values might come from contact between your congregation and one in a socialist country of Eastern Europe? Would you want to take part in such a relationship?

6. During the coming week, look for examples of people who are peacemakers—not peace lovers, but those who are doing something to *make* peace happen.

The emblem for the LWF Seventh Assembly featured an anchor—a traditional Christian symbol for hope—supporting a globe. Agota Mezösi, its creator, teaches art in a Budapest school.

Author Charles Lutz and his wife Hertha discuss an Assembly document during one of the sessions.

Appendix 1

Member Churches of the Lutheran World Federation[1]

Africa

	Baptized Membership
Cameroon	
Evangelical Lutheran Church of Cameroon	63,000
Central African Republic	
Ev. Lutheran Church of the Central African Republic	22,000
Ethiopia	
Ethiopian Evangelical Church Mekane Yesus	651,000
Evangelical Church of Eritrea	7,000
Kenya	
Evangelical Lutheran Church in Kenya	25,000
Liberia	
Lutheran Church in Liberia	26,000
Madagascar	
Malagasy Lutheran Church	600,000
Namibia	
Evangelical Lutheran Church in South-West Africa/Namibia	194,000
Evangelical Lutheran Ovambokavango Church	325,000
German Evangelical Lutheran Church in Southwest Africa[2]	12,000

1. As at close of 1984 LWF Assembly. Membership figures are those of 1984 or latest reported to LWF by member churches, rounded to nearest thousand.

Nigeria

Lutheran Church of Christ in Nigeria	63,000
Lutheran Church of Nigeria	45,000

South Africa

Evangelical Lutheran Church in Southern Africa	552,000
Evangelical Lutheran Church in Southern Africa (Cape Church)[2]	6,000
Moravian Church in Southern Africa (E. & W. Cape Province)	100,000

Tanzania

Evangelical Lutheran Church in Tanzania	1,000,000

Zimbabwe

Evangelical Lutheran Church in Zimbabwe	38,000

Africa Totals: 17 LWF member churches	3,729,000
Other Lutheran churches	144,000
	3,873,000

2. On suspended membership status by action of 1984 Assembly; see Chapter 5.

Asia

Hong Kong

Chinese Rhenish Church, Hong Kong Synod	10,000
Evangelical Lutheran Church of Hong Kong	12,000
Lutheran Church—Hong Kong Synod	6,000
Tsung Tsin Mission, Hong Kong	9,000

India

Andhra Evangelical Lutheran Church	350,000
Arcot Lutheran Church	26,000
Evangelical Lutheran Church in Madhya Pradesh	10,000
Gossner Evangelical Lutheran Church	337,000
India Evangelical Lutheran Church	56,000
Jeypore Evangelical Lutheran Church	88,000
Northern Evangelical Lutheran Church	52,000
South Andhra Lutheran Church	20,000
Tamil Evangelical Lutheran Church	88,000

Indonesia

Batak Christian Community Church	16,000
Batak Protestant Christian Church—Angkola	16,000
Christian Protestant Church in Indonesia	202,000
Indonesian Christian Church	330,000
Protestant Christian Batak Church	1,500,000
Protestant Christian Church in Mentawai	12,000
Simalungun Protestant Christian Church	155,000

Japan

Japan Evangelical Lutheran Church	20,000
Kinki Evangelical Lutheran Church	2,000

Jordan

Evangelical Lutheran Church in Jordan	2,000

Korea, Republic of

Lutheran Church in Korea	2,000

Malaysia

Basel Christian Church of Malaysia	18,000
Evangelical Lutheran Church in Malaysia and Singapore	3,000
Lutheran Church in Malaysia and Singapore	4,000

Philippines

Lutheran Church in the Philippines	17,000

Taiwan

Lutheran Church of Taiwan	1,000
Taiwan Lutheran Church	7,000

Asia Totals: 30 LWF member churches	3,373,000
Other Lutheran churches	58,000
	3,431,000

Australia—Pacific

Papua New Guinea

Evangelical Lutheran Church of Papua New Guinea	525,000
Gutnius Lutheran Church—Papua New Guinea	57,000

Australia/Pacific Totals: 2 LWF member churches	582,000
Lutheran Church of Australia	117,000
	699,000

Europe

Austria

Evangelical Church of the Augsburg Confession in Austria	379,000

Czechoslovakia

Silesian Evangelical Church of the Augsburg Confession	47,000
Slovak Evangelical Church of the Augsburg Confession	370,000

Denmark

Evangelical Lutheran Church in Denmark	5,100,000

Finland

Evangelical Lutheran Church of Finland	4,642,000

France

Church of the Augsburg Confession of Alsace & Lorraine	220,000
Evangelical Lutheran Church of France	35,000

Federal Republic of Germany

Evangelical Lutheran Church in Württemberg	2,401,000
Evangelical Lutheran Church in Baden	4,500
Evangelical Lutheran Church in Bavaria	2,562,000
Evangelical Lutheran Church in Brunswick	526,000
Evangelical Lutheran Church of Hannover	3,542,000
Evangelical Lutheran Church in Oldenburg	514,000
Evangelical Lutheran Church of Schaumburg-Lippe	70,000
North Elbian Evangelical Lutheran Church	2,767,000

German Democratic Republic

Evangelical Church of Greifswald	450,000
Evangelical Lutheran Church of Mecklenburg	700,000

Evangelical Lutheran Church of Saxony	1,800,000
Evangelical Lutheran Church in Thuringia	1,000,000

Hungary
Lutheran Church in Hungary   430,000

Iceland
National Church of Iceland   219,000

Italy
Evangelical Lutheran Church in Italy   7,000

The Netherlands
Evangelical Lutheran Church in the   30,000
   Kingdom of the Netherlands

Norway
Church of Norway   3,850,000

Poland
Evangelical Church of the Augsburg   80,000
   Confession

Romania
Evangelical Church of the Augsburg   135,000
   Confession
Synodal Evangelical Presbyterial Lutheran   30,000
   Church of the Augsburg Confession

Sweden
Church of Sweden   7,687,000

Switzerland
United Evangelical Lutheran Churches in   6,500
   Switzerland and the Principality of
   Liechtenstein

Union of Soviet Socialist Republics
Estonian Evangelical Lutheran Church   200,000
Evangelical Lutheran Church of Latvia   300,000
Evangelical Lutheran Church of Lithuania   20,000
German-speaking Lutherans   150 congregations

Yugoslavia

Evangelical Church of the Augsburg Confession	19,000
in the Socialist Republic of Slovenia	
Evangelical Church in the Socialist Republics	5,000
of Croatia, Bosnia and Herzegovnia and the Autonomous Province of Vojvodina	
Slovak Evangelical Christian Church of the Augsburg Confession in Yugoslavia	51,000

Exile Churches

Estonian Evangelical Lutheran Church in Exile	50,000
Latvian Evangelical Lutheran Church in Exile	50,000
Lithuanian Evangelical Lutheran Church in Exile	10,000

Europe Totals: 38 LWF member churches	40,125,000
Lutherans in other churches	10,344,000
	50,469,000

Latin America

Argentina

United Evangelical Lutheran Church	8,000

Bolivia

Bolivian Evangelical Lutheran Church	4,000

Brazil

Evangelical Church of the Lutheran Confession in Brazil	850,000

Chile

Evangelical Lutheran Church in Chile	2,000

Colombia

Evangelical Lutheran Church of Colombia	2,000

Guyana

Lutheran Church in Guyana	12,000

Mexico

Mexican Lutheran Church	2,000

Suriname
Evangelical Lutheran Church in Suriname   4,000

Latin America Totals: 8 LWF member churches	884,000
Other Lutheran churches	317,000
	1,201,000

North America

Canada
Evangelical Lutheran Church of Canada[3]   85,000
Lutheran Church in America, Canada Section[3]   125,000

United States of America
American Lutheran Church[4]   2,342,000
Association of Evangelical Lutheran Churches[4]   111,000
Lutheran Church in America[4]   2,925,000

N. America Totals: 4 LWF member churches	5,588,000
Members of exile churches	24,000
Other Lutheran churches	3,208,000
	8,820,000

World Totals: 99 LWF member churches	54,397,000
Lutherans in other churches	14,096,000
	68,493,000

3. ELCC and LCA Canada Section expect to unite by 1986 into the Evangelical Lutheran Church in Canada, a church of approximately 210,000 members.
4. The three U.S. member churches expect to unite by 1988 into a new church of approximately 5,400,000 members.

Appendix 2

Message from the Seventh Assembly of the Lutheran World Federation to the Lutheran Churches throughout the World

"May the God of hope fill you with all joy and peace in believing, so that by the power of the Holy Spirit you may abound in hope."

We, delegates to the Assembly, send you these words from Romans 15:13 as a token of our experience during the two weeks when we worshiped, studied and deliberated around the theme "In Christ—Hope for the World."

We saw a sign of that hope in our coming together from all parts of the world as Lutherans who share in a common confession of faith in Christ. Meeting in Budapest, Hungary, the Federation was assembling for the first time in a socialist country in Eastern Europe. Our gathering here and the hospitality we received here showed us that in the church of Christ we can have confidence in each other and can build bridges between people across political and ideological boundaries.

Unity in word and sacrament

This Assembly affirmed more explicitly than ever the unity the member churches have in communion at the altar and in the proclamation of God's Word from the pulpit. It looked beyond its own community to the recent growth in visible unity with other churches. As theological convergence occurs, there has developed an urgency to translate the results into the practical life and relationships of churches and congregations.

In the world and in the church, unity and hope are often clouded by inequality and tension between North and South, between women and men, between generations and between races. In the Assembly agreement was sometimes difficult to achieve. Remembering that in Christ there is neither Jew nor Greek, slave nor free, male nor female, our hope grew for an inclusive church where the gifts of all are precious and where all share a ministry for the life of the world as commissioned in baptism. The presence of youth provided a hopeful sign and convinced us they must have full participation in the church.

When we heard of children eating wet paper to take away pangs of hunger, we were reminded that some of us lived in neighborhoods of relative luxury and self-indulgence, while others came from areas where millions exist on the edge of starvation. God's creation is being despoiled to provide superabundance for some. Poverty threatens survival and increases a population explosion in many places. Privation and oppression drive some to wars of liberation. Resources are wasted on other wars, the arms trade and an escalating arms race amid heightened tensions between East and West that make a mockery of security and threaten life in the world with nuclear holocaust.

So we turned to the resources of our faith as all must do in the congregations of the churches. There is no time for despair nor carelessness. Where there are restrictions on human rights and violations against the dignity of persons, we call for and pledge to work for freedom to express one's conscience without fear. Where poverty presses people into subhuman conditions, we commit ourselves to learn better the meaning of being created in the image of God and we will not only expand direct help that enables others to help themselves, but we will work for a world of more equitable and just political and economic systems. We will learn again God's command to care for the creation. Encouraged by God's act of reconciliation by Jesus Christ, we will not settle for self-satisfied nationalism but we will pray for better relations among all peoples. We will exercise our Christian love to join with reasonable people who desire well-being in the whole world and work to enhance the hope for peace. So we hope to grow in unity of love and service as well as in faith.

However, falling short of perfection, beset by sin, threatened by demonic evil, we survive only by faith. Christian hope is not founded in our own strength; it is grounded on the acts of God. Christ offered himself on the cross for all people and God raised him from the dead. The Holy Spirit empowered the church to witness to the good news through the ages, until it has reached us. Now we are called to mission.

Universal call to mission

Recognizing that mission is central to the life of the church, and hearing of the multitude who have not received the gospel, we call the churches to engage in joint action in mission, and, with their congregations, to intensify mission outreach locally and around the world. We rejoice in every opportunity to proclaim the gospel freely, and we suffer with those who are restrained. We are not called to be a mirror of our society, but to be salt and light. As we identify with the people in the world, we commit ourselves to servanthood under the sign of Christ's cross. We, and all in Christian congregations everywhere, have the privilege of being children of hope. We confess that our Lord Jesus will return in glory and we pray with all Christians, "Amen. Come, Lord Jesus!" (Rev. 22:20).

"And the peace of God, which passes all understanding, will keep your hearts and your minds in Christ Jesus" (Phil. 4:7).

Appendix 3

Background Materials on the Seventh Assembly

These materials are available as aids for interpreting the Seventh Assembly of the Lutheran World Federation. All are in English and prices are in U.S. dollars.

From Geneva: LWF Communication Department
Box 66, CH-1211
Geneva 20, Switzerland

- Official Proceedings of the Seventh Assembly, in LWF Report series (including presentations and responses, general secretary's report, official Assembly statements, working group reports and Assembly actions, revised LWF constitution, list of new Executive Committee and Commission members).
- Assembly Bible studies, *Our Hope in Christ*, LWF Documentation, no. 14, $5.
- Seven-year report, *From Dar es Salaam to Budapest*, LWF Report, no. 17/18, $10.
- 50-minute audiocassette providing Assembly highlights, $8.
- Slide program (60 slides) with script (English or German), $30.
- "In Christ Hope," 25-minute color film or videocassette, links Assembly to everyday life of Lutheran churches. (Ask for rental or purchase prices.)
- Black and white photos of Assembly events. (Ask for prices.)

From New York: Lutheran World Ministries
Office of Communication
360 Park Avenue South
New York, NY 10010
tel. 212/532-6350

- 28-minute videotape, "Voice of the Prophets: LWF Assembly." VHS copies are available on free-loan basis from district/synod resource centers in U.S. and Canada. Three-quarter inch and beta copies available for sale or loan from Lutheran World Ministries.
- Assembly preparatory materials:
Theme book, "In Christ—Hope for the World," LWF Documentation, no. 13, $3.80.
- Issue material for working groups, "Signs of Hope," LWF Documentation, no. 15/16, $9.
- Bible studies, "Our Hope in Christ" (see above), also available from Lutheran World Ministries, $5.

From Sweden: Utryck Publishing
Faalhagsleden 8A
S-75324
Uppsala, Sweden

- 14 songs of protest and praise from South Africa, "Freedom Is Coming," by Swedish singing group Fjedur, which performed at the Seventh Assembly; book of song in four-part harmony with words and pictures about the struggle for freedom in South Africa, $8; sound cassette, $5.

Appendix 4

Structure of the LWF

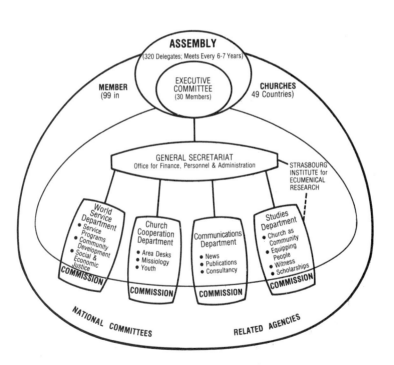

Notes

1. Who Are the Members of This Family?

1. Augsburg Confession, Art. 7.
2. There are 520,000 Lutherans in organized churches in the Soviet republics of Estonia, Latvia, and Lithuania. Approximately 150 congregations exist also in republics east of the Urals, such as Kazakhstan and Uzbek. These German-speaking people, relocated there from the Ukraine and the Volga region during World War II, are not organized into a church body, and therefore membership figures are imprecise.
3. For complete list of LWF member churches, see Appendix 1.
4. Close partners of LWF World Service in global programs of material aid are two North American Lutheran agencies: Lutheran World Relief in the U.S. and Canadian Lutheran World Relief. Both agencies represent most Lutheran churches of their countries, including the LWF member churches and the Lutheran Church–Missouri Synod. Both carry out part of their international aid programs—combating hunger, assisting refugees, and providing emergency service—through LWF's World Service Department.
5. Presidents of the LWF function as the visible and symbolic heads of world Lutheranism. The seven who have held that office, and the assemblies at which they were elected, are: Professor Anders Nygren of Sweden—Lund, 1947; Bishop Hanns Lilje of West Germany—Hannover, 1952; President Franklin Clark Fry of the U.S.—Minneapolis, 1957; President Fredrik A. Schiotz of the U.S.—Helsinki, 1963; Bishop Mikko Juva of Finland—Evian, 1970; Bishop Josiah Kibira of Tanzania—Dar es Salaam, 1977; Bishop Zoltan Kaldy of Hungary—Budapest, 1984.

2. What Gives the Family Hope?

1. Josiah Kibira, Tanzanian bishop, in address to the LWF Executive Committee, 1982.
2. Klaus-Peter Hertzsch, keynote address to LWF Budapest Assembly, July 23, 1984.
3. *Study Book for the Seventh LWF Assembly*, LWF Documentation, no. 13 (September 1983), p. 22.

4. "Message from the Seventh Assembly of the Lutheran World Federation, 1984, to the Lutheran Churches throughout the World." Full text appears as Appendix 2 in this book.

5. *Study Book for the Seventh LWF Assembly*, p. 26.

6. Carl E. Braaten, *Christ and Counter-Christ* (Philadelphia: Fortress, 1972), p. 69; quoted in *Study Book.*

7. Yoshiro Ishida, "Imperatives and Openings for World Mission and Evangelism," *Dialog* 22 (no. 2, 1983): 135.

8. *Study Book*, p. 47.

3. What Is the Family's Task?

1. Erika Schuchardt, *Warum gerade ich . . . ? Behinderung und Glaube* (Gelnhausen/Berling, 1981 and 1984), p. 91.

2. "Working Paper on Mission," received by the LWF Seventh Assembly, Budapest, 1984. Available from Lutheran World Federation Communication Department, Route de Ferney 150, P.O. Box 66, 1211 Geneva 20, Switzerland.

3. Available from World Association for Christian Communication, 122 King's Road, London SW3 4TR, England. Articles on "Christian Communication Today" are available in a March 1984 LWF Documentation publication. Order from LWF Communication Department, Route de Ferney 150, P.O. Box 66, 1211 Geneva 20, Switzerland.

4. Both are available from LWF Studies Department, Route de Ferney 150, P.O. Box 66, 1211 Geneva 20, Switzerland.

5. There are some countries in which the churches are not permitted to engage in ministries of education or service in the society, but Word and sacrament ministries are allowed. Then everything must center in worship, including catechetics and communication about the faith community's work and witness in the world. The church gathered for worship in such situations becomes the *only* integrating reality.

6. Participants from India in the Budapest working group discussions on worship shared how common worship in their situation has a strong witness role in relation to the surrounding non-Christian population.

4. How Does the Family Relate to Other Families?

1. "In Christ—a New Community." Proceedings of the Sixth Assembly of the LWF, 1977, pp. 173-75.

2. On U.S. bilateral dialogues, "Lutherans in Ecumenical Dialogue: an Interpretive Guide" is provided by Lutheran Council in the USA, 360 Park Ave. S., New York, NY 10010. An updated version was in preparation at the beginning of 1985.

3. "Baptism, Eucharist and Ministry" has been shared with Lutheran congregations of member churches of the World Council of Churches in the United States and Canada. Copies may also be purchased in certain religious bookstores or from Friendship Press, 475 Riverside Drive, New York, NY 10115.

4. From report of working group on BEM, Budapest Assembly of the LWF.

5. "Growth in Ecumenical Commitment" is available from Lutheran World Ministries, 360 Park Ave. S., New York, NY 10010.

6. "Common Witness and Proselytism: a Study Document" (from a joint commission of the World Council of Churches and the Roman Catholic church), in *Ecumenical Review* 23 (1971): 9; see also pp. 15-17.

7. Available from Lutheran World Ministries, 360 Park Ave. S., New York, NY 10010.

5. How Does the Family Maintain Its Unity?

1. Amendments to the LWF constitution are officially in effect one year after the close of an assembly (thus, August 1985 in the case of the Budapest amendments), unless there is objection from at least one-third (currently 33) of its member churches.

2. The two reports are available from Lutheran World Ministries, 360 Park Ave. S., New York, NY 10010.

3. In a presentation at the North American pre-Assembly consultation, Ypsilanti, Michigan, March 1984. See also Bertram's article in *The Debate on Status Confessionis: Studies in Christian Political Theology* (Geneva: LWF Department of Studies, 1983).

6. Who Gives Leadership to the Family?

1. The LWF executive committee, meeting immediately after the Budapest Assembly, elected women to chair three of the four LWF Commissions: Communication (Ruth Abraham of Ethiopia), Church Cooperation (Dorothy Marple of the United

States), and Studies (Christina Berglund of Sweden). An Indian male bishop, Munshi N. Tudu, was chosen to chair World Service.

2. "Women in the Ministries of the Church," December 1983; May 1984 issue of *Women*—both available from LWF Studies Department, Route de Ferney 150, P.O. Box 66, 1211, Geneva 20, Switzerland.

3. "Women in the Ministries of the Church," p. 27.

4. Data gathered in late 1980 indicated that, in Lutheran churches ordaining women, approximately 6% of the pastors were women. The same survey reported that 29% of those churches' theology students were women. While women's ordination was first practiced by some Lutheran churches in Europe nearly 60 years ago, it has come to other continents only in the past two decades, to some Asian and African churches in the 1960s, and to North America in 1970. Today, Australia is the only continent with no ordained Lutheran women (*Women*, May 1984 issue, LWF Studies Department).

7. How Shall the Family Live Amid Poverty and Wealth?

1. Figures are for 1983, as reported in the World Bank's "1984 World Development Report." The 1983 figure for Norway is 1.1% (1st among all nations), for the Netherlands, .91%, and for Sweden, .88%. The Netherlands and Sweden were slightly over 1.0% in 1982. The United States had as much as 2.9% of its GNP in economic assistance during peak years of the Marshall Plan in the late 1940s, but has been far below 1.0% in recent decades.

2. A helpful book on the themes of economic justice is *Mirror or Model* by Sibusiso Bengu, the South African political economist who directs the Office of Research and Social Action for LWF World Service. Copies may be ordered from Lutheran World Ministries, 360 Park Ave. S., New York, NY 10010.

3. Grape-Lantz is deputy general secretary of the International Center of the Swedish Labor Movement; her comment was part of her response to Carl von Weizsaecker's Assembly address on peace.

8. How Shall the Family Work for Peace in the World?

1. George Kennan in an essay, "On Nuclear War," in his book *Nuclear Delusion* (Pantheon, 1982), p. 199.

2. The Lutherans of Czechoslovakia (Slovak Evangelical Church of the Augsburg Confession) have identified with a similar theological position. The Slovaks and Hungarians jointly published a theological study titled "In Christ—Hope for the World" and made it available to Assembly delegates (Press Department, Lutheran Church in Hungary, Deak Ter 4, 1052 Budapest, Hungary). Other eastern European Lutheran churches, notably those in the German Democratic Republic, have taken somewhat different stances in relation to their social order.

3. Staalsett, general secretary of the Norwegian Bible Society since 1982, was elected in early February 1985 as the sixth general secretary of the LWF. He succeeds Carl H. Mau Jr., an American Lutheran Church pastor, in the LWF's top staff position on September 1, 1985. Staalsett, born in 1935, has served as a youth pastor, lecturer in systematic theology, and was general secretary of the Church of Norway's Council of Foreign Relations, 1970-77.